Q: Skills for Success

LISTENING AND SPEAKING

INTRO

Kevin McClure

Mari Vargo

SERIES CONSULTANTS

Marguerite Ann Snow

Lawrence J. Zwier

VOCABULARY CONSULTANT

Cheryl Boyd Zimmerman

OXFORD
UNIVERSITY PRESS

OXFORD
UNIVERSITY PRESS

198 Madison Avenue

New York, NY 10016 USA

Great Clarendon Street, Oxford, OX2 6DP, United Kingdom

Oxford University Press is a department of the University of Oxford.
It furthers the University's objective of excellence in research, scholarship,
and education by publishing worldwide. Oxford is a registered trade
mark of Oxford University Press in the UK and in certain other countries.

General Manager, American ELT: Laura Pearson
Publisher: Stephanie Karras
Associate Publishing Manager: Sharon Sargent
Senior Development Editor: Andrew Gitzy
Associate Development Editors: Rebecca Mostov, Keyana Shaw
Director, ADP: Susan Sanguily
Executive Design Manager: Maj-Britt Hagsted
Associate Design Manager: Michael Steinhofer
Electronic Production Manager: Julie Armstrong
Production Artist: Elissa Santos
Cover Design: Molly Scanlon
Image Manager: Trisha Masterson
Image Editor: Liaht Pashayan
Production Coordinator: Elizabeth Matsumoto

ISBN: 978-0-19-475646-4 LISTENING AND SPEAKING INTRO
STUDENT BOOK PACK

ISBN: 978-0-19-475649-5 LISTENING AND SPEAKING INTRO
STUDENT BOOK

ISBN: 978-0-19-475621-1 Q ONLINE PRACTICE
STUDENT ACCESS CODE CARD

Printed in China

This book is printed on paper from certified and well-managed sources.

ACKNOWLEDGEMENTS

The publishers would like to thank the following for their kind permission to reproduce photographs:
Cover John Giustina/Iconica/Getty Images; Sean Justice/Riser/Getty Images; Kirsty
Pargeter/iStockphoto; Leontura/iStockphoto; Illustrious/iStockphoto; vi Marcin Krygier/
iStockphoto; xiii Rüstem Gürler/iStockphoto; p. 2 Solent News & Photo Agency/Rex/Rex
USA; p. 4 Image Source/Corbis; p. 5 PhotoAlto/Alamy; p. 7 Jim West/age fotostock;
p. 8 Radius Images/Corbis; p. 11 Tony West/Corbis; p. 13 Twentieth Century-Fox Film
Corporation/the Kobal Collection; p. 14 David Pu'u/Corbis; p. 18 David R. Gee/Alamy;
p. 21 Jim West/age fotostock (food bank); p. 21 Petrenko Andriy/shutterstock.com (lying
in grass); p. 21 Ocean/Corbis (college class); p. 21 Chris Howes/Wild Places Photography/
Alamy (beach); p. 21 Custom Medical Stock Photo/Alamy (therapist); p. 24 Glow Asia RF/
Alamy; p. 26 Yuri Arcurs/Alamy; p. 28 Ocean/Corbis; p. 29 photofriday/shutterstock.com
(tennis); p. 29 robfood/Alamy (cooking); p. 32 Blend Images/Alamy; p. 35 AP Photo/Carolyn
Kaster; p. 37 Purestock/SuperStock/Corbis; p. 40 Rick Friedman/Corbis; p. 41 Jim Rogash/
WireImage/Getty Images; p. 42 Frederick Bass/fstop/Corbis; p. 43 Peter Christopher/
Masterfile; p. 44 Bob Peterson/Getty Images; p. 46 Mira/Alamy; p. 48 Adrianna Williams/
Corbis; p. 49 Daly and Newton/Getty Images; p. 50 Ariel Skelley/Getty Images; p. 51
Photodisc/Oxford University Press; p. 53 G. Biss/Masterfile; p. 56 Image Source/Getty
Images; p. 60 James Appleton/Alamy; p. 62 Eddy Risch/epa/Corbis (painting); p. 62 All
Canada Photos/SuperStock (sculptures); p. 62 Marcus Brandt/epa/Corbis (orchestra);
p. 62 Masterfile (barbeque); p. 62 Manuel Fernandes/shutterstock.com (path); p. 62 Richard
Cummins/SuperStock (wildflowers); p. 62 Don Emmert/AFP/Getty Images (crowd); p. 62
JGI/Blend Images/Corbis (reading); p. 63 Carlos Alkmin/Getty Images; p. 64 Marka/Alamy;
p. 65 Blend Images/Alamy; p. 66 Henry Westheim Photography/Alamy (kickboxing); p. 66
Aurora Photos/Masterfile (skiing); p. 69 Photononstop/SuperStock; p. 70 Mike Goldwater/
Alamy; p. 71 Doug Menuez/Getty Images (basketball); p. 71 Graham French/Masterfile
(movies); p. 72 Asia Images/Getty Images (man at desk); p. 72 Ciaran Griffin/Getty Images
(woman with backpack); p. 76 Della Huff/Alamy; p. 79 Stock Connection/SuperStock
(house); p. 79 Yellow Dog Productions/Getty Images (dorm room); p. 79 PhotoStock-Israel/
Alamy (studio apartment); p. 82 J. LL. Banús/age fotostock; p. 84 Frances Roberts/Alamy (for
rent sign); p. 84 Kazuhiro Nogi/AFP/Getty Images (man giving speech); p. 85 Russell Kord/
Alamy; p. 86 Konstantin L/shutterstock.com; p. 87 Steve Heap/shutterstock.com (pool);
p. 87 Image Source/Corbis (fireplace); p. 94 Don Emmert/AFP/Getty Images; p. 96 Peter
Casolino/Alamy; p. 97 Stockbyte/Oxford University Press; p. 99 Yellow Dog Productions/
Getty Images; p. 100 Atli Mar Hafsteinsson/Masterfile (bike path); p. 100 Hemis.fr/
SuperStock (desert); p. 102 Jim Reed/Corbis (fog); p. 102 Aflo Relax/Masterfile (spring
trees); p. 102 Yuriy Kulyk/shutterstock.com (green field); p. 102 Photodisc/Oxford
University Press (autumn forest); p. 102 Ellen Rooney/Robert Harding World Imagery/
Corbis (winter); p. 103 BananaStock/Oxford University Press; p. 104 Christer Fredriksson/
Getty Images; p. 107 Purcell-Holmes/Getty Images; p. 109 Gene Blevins/LA Daily News/
Corbis (lightning); p. 109 age fotostock/SuperStock (rainbow); p. 112 Drive Images/
age fotostock; p. 114 Klaus Mellenthin/Getty Images; p. 115 Marka/SuperStock
(sphygmomanometer); p. 115 Chris Rout/Alamy (stressed woman); p. 116 Hill Street
Studios/Getty Images; p. 119 Atlantide Phototravel/Corbis; p. 121 Asia Images/SuperStock;
p. 122 David Buffington/Getty Images; p. 123 Chase Jarvis/Getty Images; p. 125 Charles
Thatcher/Getty Images; p. 130 Marco Simoni/Getty Images; p. 132 Cat Gwynn/Corbis;
p. 133 Maugli/shutterstock.com (Rome); p. 133 Matej Pavlansky/shutterstock.com
(airplane); p. 133 Michael Yamashita/Corbis (New York); p. 133 Pixtal Images/photolibrary
(Bali); p. 133 Didier Bergounhoux/Photononstop/photolibrary (Belgium); p. 134 Bob Krist/
Corbis; 135 Fuse/Oxford University Press; p. 136 Photodisc/Oxford University Press
(blueprint); p. 136 Napa Valley Register/J.L. Sousa/ZUMA Press/Corbis (town hall meeting);
p. 137 René Mansi/istockphoto.com; p. 139 HBSS/Corbis (architectual model); p. 139
Robert Harding Picture Library Ltd/Alamy (Thailand restaurant); p. 142 Tibor Bognár/age
fotostock; p. 143 Fancy/Alamy; p. 144 Goodshoot/Oxford University Press; p. 144
Hiroyuki Matsumoto/Getty Images (Mexico City); p. 145 Travelshots.com/Alamy (Globe
Theater), (Oxford Street); p. 145 Grant Rooney PCL/SuperStock (British Museum); 145 Rudy
Sulgan/Corbis (Trafalgar Square); p. 145 Photodisc/Oxford University Press (Tower of
London); p. 148 Everett Kennedy Brown/epa/Corbis; p. 150 Asia Images/Masterfile
(chalkboard); p. 150 Jeff Greenberg/Alamy (spelling bee); p. 151 Mike Agliolo/Corbis (light
bulb); p. 151 Courtesy of Ania Filochowska (Ania Filochowska); p. 153 Jim Powell/Alamy;
p. 154 ColorBlind/Getty Images (supermarket manager); p. 154 Erik Dreyer/Getty Images
(library); p. 155 Rightdisc/Alamy (pen); p. 155 epa/Corbis (Naguib Mahfouz); p. 158 Ron
Koeberer/Getty Images; p. 160 REB Images/Blend Images/Corbis (car keys); p. 160 Fancy/
Alamy (cell phone); p. 162 Tim Ayers/Alamy; p. 163 Campus Life/Getty Images.

Illustrations by: p. 5 Greg Paprocki; p. 16 Stacy Merlin; p. 23 Barb Bastian; p. 35 Karen Minot;
p. 38 Stacy Merlin; p. 49 Greg Paprocki; p. 52 Barb Bastian; p. 54 Stuart Bradford; p. 57
Barb Bastian; p. 63 Karen Minot; p. 67 Stuart Bradford; p. 79 Karen Minot; p. 81 Karen
Minot; p. 89 Karen Minot; p. 92 Karen Minot; p. 97 Karen Minot; p. 101 Karen Minot;
p. 117 Greg Paprocki; p. 118 Stacy Merlin; p. 120 Greg Paprocki; p. 127 Barb Bastian;
p. 137 Stacy Merlin; p. 145 Stacy Merlin; p. 157 Stuart Bradford.

ACKNOWLEDGEMENTS

Authors

Kevin McClure holds an M.A. in Applied Linguistics from the University of South Florida and has taught English in the United States, France, and Japan. In addition to his extensive teaching experience, he served as the Academic Director at the ELS Language Center in San Francisco for eight years. He developed both print and online ESL/EFL materials. His main interests are computer-aided language learning and teaching conversation management skills to low-level students.

Mari Vargo holds an M.A. in English from San Francisco State University. She has taught numerous ESL courses at the university level. She has also written textbooks and online course materials for a wide range of programs, including community colleges, universities, corporations, and primary and secondary schools.

Series Consultants

Marguerite Ann Snow holds a Ph.D. in Applied Linguistics from UCLA. She is a Professor in the Charter College of Education at California State University, Los Angeles where she teaches in the TESOL M.A. program. She has published in *TESOL Quarterly, Applied Linguistics*, and *The Modern Language Journal*. She has been a Fulbright scholar in Hong Kong and Cyprus. In 2006, she received the President's Distinguished Professor award at Cal State LA. In addition to working closely with ESL and mainstream public school teachers in the U.S., she has trained EFL teachers in Algeria, Argentina, Brazil, Egypt, Japan, Morocco, Pakistan, Spain, and Turkey. Her main interests are integrated content and language instruction, English for Academic Purposes, and standards for English teaching and learning.

Lawrence J. Zwier holds an M.A. in TESL from the University of Minnesota. He is currently the Associate Director for Curriculum Development at the English Language Center at Michigan State University in East Lansing. He has taught ESL/EFL in the U.S., Saudi Arabia, Malaysia, Japan, and Singapore. He is a frequent TESOL conference presenter and has published many ESL/EFL books in the areas of test-preparation, vocabulary, and reading, including *Inside Reading 2* for Oxford University Press.

Vocabulary Consultant

Cheryl Boyd Zimmerman is Associate Professor of TESOL at California State University, Fullerton. She specializes in second-language vocabulary acquisition, an area in which she is widely published. She teaches graduate courses on second-language acquisition, culture, vocabulary, and the fundamentals of TESOL and is a frequent invited speaker on topics related to vocabulary teaching and learning. She is the author of *Word Knowledge: A Vocabulary Teacher's Handbook* and Series Director of *Inside Reading*, both published by Oxford University Press.

Special thanks to our Introductory level advisors:

Aftab Ahmed, American University of Sharjah, U.A.E.; **Grace Bishop**, Houston Community College, TX; **Dr. İlke Büyükduman**, Istanbul Şehir University, Turkey; **Julie Carey**, American Language Institute, CA; **Pauline Koyess Chahine**, Qatar Armed Forces Language School, Qatar; **Yuwen Catherine Chen**, Eden English, Taichung; **Marta Dmytrenko-Ahrabian**, Wayne State University, MI; **Angela Donovan**, Language Studies International, NY; **Joan Fiser**, Sequoia High School, CA; **Kathleen Golata**, Galileo Academy, CA; **Janet Harclerode**, Santa Monica College, CA; **Hassan Hawash**, Abu Dhabi Men's College, U.A.E.; **Hui-min Hung**, Hot English School, Kaohsiung; **Mark Landa**, Mukogawa Women's University, Japan; **Renee LaRue**, Lone Star College-Montgomery, TX; **Janet Langon**, Glendale Community College, CA; **Paula Lee**, West Valley-Mission Community College District, CA; **Amy Ma**, Hot English School, Kaohsiung; **Neil McBeath**, Sultan Qaboos University, Oman; **Gorgan Myles**, Momoyama Gakuin Daigaku, Japan; **Ahmed Ra'ef**, Saudi Academy, Saudi Arabia; **Leslie Ramirez**, Pasadena Memorial High School, TX; **Richard Seltzer**, Glendale Community College, CA; **Yusuf Şen**, Düzce University, Turkey; **Christine Tierney**, Houston Community College, TX; **Nathan Vasarhely**, Ygnacio Valley High School, CA; **Robert Wenn**, Abu Dhabi Men's College; U.A.E.

REVIEWERS

We would like to acknowledge the advice of teachers from all over the world who participated in online reviews, focus groups, and editorial reviews. We relied heavily on teacher input throughout the extensive development process of the Q series, and many of the features in the series came directly from feedback we gathered from teachers in the classroom. We are grateful to all who helped.

UNITED STATES Marcarena Aguilar, North Harris College, TX; Deborah Anholt, Lewis and Clark College, OR; Robert Anzelde, Oakton Community College, IL; Arlys Arnold, University of Minnesota, MN; Marcia Arthur, Renton Technical College, WA; Anne Bachmann, Clackamas Community College, OR; Ron Balsamo, Santa Rosa Junior College, CA; Lori Barkley, Portland State University, OR; Eileen Barlow, SUNY Albany, NY; Sue Bartch, Cuyahoga Community College, OH; Lora Bates, Oakton High School, VA; Nancy Baum, University of Texas at Arlington, TX; Linda Berendsen, Oakton Community College, IL; Jennifer Binckes Lee, Howard Community College, MD; Grace Bishop, Houston Community College, TX; Jean W. Bodman, Union County College, NJ; Virginia Bouchard, George Mason University, VA; Kimberley Briesch Sumner, University of Southern California, CA; Gabriela Cambiasso, Harold Washington College, IL; Jackie Campbell, Capistrano Unified School District, CA; Adele C. Camus, George Mason University, VA; Laura Chason, Savannah College, GA; Kerry Linder Catana, Language Studies International, NY; An Cheng, Oklahoma State University, OK; Carole Collins, North Hampton Community College, PA; Betty R. Compton, Intercultural Communications College, HI; Pamela Couch, Boston University, MA; Fernanda Crowe, Intrax International Institute, CA; Margo Czinski, Washtenaw Community College, MI; David Dahnke, Lone Star College, TX; Gillian M. Dale, CA; L. Dalgish, Concordia College, MN; Christopher Davis, John Jay College, NY; Sonia Delgadillo, Sierra College, CA; Marta O. Dmytrenko-Ahrabian, Wayne State University, MI; Javier Dominguez, Central High School, SC; Jo Ellen Downey-Greer, Lansing Community College, MI; Jennifer Duclos, Boston University, MA; Yvonne Duncan, City College of San Francisco, CA; Jennie Farnell, University of Connecticut, CT; Susan Fedors, Howard Community College, MD; Matthew Florence, Intrax International Institute, CA; Kathleen Flynn, Glendale College, CA; Eve Fonseca, St. Louis Community College, MO; Elizabeth Foss, Washtenaw Community College, MI; Duff C. Galda, Pima Community College, AZ; Christiane Galvani, Houston Community College, TX; Gretchen Gerber, Howard Community College, MD; Ray Gonzalez, Montgomery College, MD; Alyona Gorokhova, Grossmont College, CA; John Graney, Santa Fe College, FL; Kathleen Green, Central High School, AZ; Webb Hamilton, De Anza College, San Jose City College, CA; Janet Harclerode, Santa Monica Community College, CA; Sandra Hartmann, Language and Culture Center, TX; Kathy Haven, Mission College, CA; Adam Henricksen, University of Maryland, MD; Peter Hoffman, LaGuardia Community College, NY; Linda Holden, College of Lake County, IL; Jana Holt, Lake Washington Technical College, WA; Gail Ibele, University of Wisconsin, WI; Mandy Kama, Georgetown University, Washington, DC; Stephanie Kasuboski, Cuyahoga Community College, OH; Chigusa Katoku, Mission College, CA; Sandra Kawamura, Sacramento City College, CA; Gail Kellersberger, University of Houston–Downtown, TX; Jane Kelly, Durham Technical Community College, NC; Julie Park Kim, George Mason University, VA; Lisa Kovacs-Morgan University of California, San Diego, CA; Claudia Kupiec, DePaul University, IL; Renee La Rue, Lone Star College-Montgomery, TX; Janet Langon, Glendale College, CA; Lawrence Lawson, Palomar College, CA; Rachele Lawton, The Community College of Baltimore County, MD; Alice Lee, Richland College, TX; Cherie Lenz-Hackett, University of Washington, WA; Joy Leventhal, Cuyahoga Community College, OH; Candace Lynch-Thompson, North Orange County Community College District, CA; Thi Thi Ma, City College of San Francisco, CA; Denise Maduli-Williams, City College of San Francisco, CA; Eileen Mahoney, Camelback High School, AZ; Brigitte Maronde, Harold Washington College, IL; Keith Maurice, University of Texas at Arlington, TX; Nancy Mayer, University of Missouri-St. Louis, MO; Karen Merritt, Glendale Union High School District, AZ; Holly Milkowart, Johnson County Community College, KS; Eric Moyer, Intrax International Institute, CA; Gino Muzzatti, Santa Rosa Junior College, CA; William Nedrow, Triton College, IL; Eric Nelson, University of Minnesota, MN; Rhony Ory, Ygnacio Valley High School, CA; Paul Parent, Montgomery College, MD; Oscar Pedroso, Miami Dade College, FL; Robin Persiani, Sierra College, CA; Patricia Prenz-Belkin, Hostos Community College, NY; Jim Ranalli, Iowa State University, IA; Toni R. Randall, Santa Monica College, CA; Vidya Rangachari, Mission College, CA; Elizabeth Rasmussen, Northern Virginia Community College, VA; Lara Ravitch, Truman College, IL; Deborah Repasz, San Jacinto College, TX; Andrey Reznikov, Black Hills State University, SD; Alison Rice, Hunter College, NY; Jennifer Robles, Ventura Unified School District, CA; Priscilla Rocha, Clark County School District, NV; Dzidra Rodins, DePaul University IL; Maria Rodriguez, Central High School, AZ; Maria Ruiz, Victor Valley College, CA; Kimberly Russell, Clark College, WA; Irene Sakk, Northwestern University, IL; Shaeley Santiago, Ames High School, IA; Peg Sarosy, San Francisco State University, CA; Alice Savage, North Harris College, TX; Donna Schaeffer, University of Washington, WA; Carol Schinger, Northern Virginia Community College, VA; Robert Scott, Kansas State University, KS; Suell Scott, Sheridan Technical Center, FL; Shira Seaman, Global English Academy, NY; Richard Seltzer, Glendale Community College, CA; Kathy Sherak, San Francisco State University, CA; German Silva, Miami Dade College, FL; Andrea Spector, Santa Monica Community College, CA; Karen Stanely, Central Piedmont Community College, NC; Ayse Stromsdorfer, Soldan I.S.H.S., MO; Yilin Sun, South Seattle Community College, WA; Thomas Swietlik, Intrax International Institute, IL; Judith Tanka, UCLA Extension–American Language Center, CA; Priscilla Taylor, University of Southern California, CA; Ilene Teixeira, Fairfax County Public Schools, VA; Shirl H. Terrell, Collin College, TX; Marya Teutsch-Dwyer, St. Cloud State University, MN; Stephen Thergesen, ELS Language Centers, CO; Christine Tierney, Houston Community College, TX; Arlene Turini, North Moore High School, NC; Suzanne Van Der Valk, Iowa State University, IA; Nathan D. Vasarhely, Ygnacio Valley High School, CA; Naomi S. Verratti, Howard Community College, MD; Hollyahna Vettori, Santa Rosa Junior College, CA; Julie Vorholt, Lewis & Clark College, OR; Laura Walsh, City College of San Francisco, CA; Andrew J. Watson, The English Bakery; Donald Weasenforth, Collin College, TX; Juliane Widner, Sheepshead Bay High School, NY; Lynne Wilkins, Mills College, CA; Dolores "Lorrie" Winter, California State University at Fullerton, CA; Jody Yamamoto, Kapi'olani Community College, HI; Ellen L. Yaniv, Boston University, MA; Norman Yoshida, Lewis & Clark College, OR; Joanna Zadra, American River College, CA; Florence Zysman, Santiago Canyon College, CA;

ASIA Rabiatu Abubakar, Eton Language Centre, Malaysia; Wiwik Andreani, Bina Nusantara University, Indonesia; Mike Baker, Kosei Junior High School, Japan; Leonard Barrow, Kanto Junior College, Japan; Herman Bartelen, Japan; Siren Betty, Fooyin University, Kaohsiung; Thomas E. Bieri, Nagoya College, Japan; Natalie Brezden, Global English House, Japan; MK Brooks, Mukogawa Women's University, Japan; Truong Ngoc Buu, The Youth Language School, Vietnam; Charles Cabell, Toyo University, Japan; Fred Carruth, Matsumoto University, Japan; Frances Causer, Seijo University, Japan; Deborah Chang, Wenzao Ursuline College of Languages, Kaohsiung; David Chatham, Ritsumeikan University, Japan; Andrew Chih Hong Chen, National Sun Yat-sen University, Kaohsiung; Christina Chen, Yu-Tsai Bilingual Elementary School, Taipei; Jason Jeffree Cole, Coto College, Japan; Le Minh Cong, Vungtau Tourism Vocational College, Vietnam; Todd Cooper, Toyama National College of Technology, Japan; Marie Cosgrove, Daito Bunka University, Japan; Tony Cripps, Ritsumeikan University, Japan; Daniel Cussen, Takushoku University, Japan; Le Dan, Ho Chi Minh City Electric Power College, Vietnam; Simon Daykin, Banghwa-dong Community Centre, South Korea; Aimee Denham, ILA, Vietnam; Bryan Dickson, David's English Center, Taipei; Nathan Ducker, Japan University, Japan; Ian Duncan, Simul International Corporate Training, Japan; Nguyen Thi Kieu Dung, Thang Long University, Vietnam; Nguyen Thi Thuy Duong, Vietnamese American Vocational Training College, Vietnam; Wong Tuck Ee, Raja Tun Azlan Science Secondary School, Malaysia; Emilia Effendy, International Islamic University Malaysia, Malaysia; Robert Eva, Kaisei Girls High School, Japan; Jim George, Luna International Language School, Japan; Jurgen Germeys, Silk Road Language Center, South Korea; Wong Ai Gnoh, SMJK Chung Hwa Confucian, Malaysia; Peter Goosselink, Hokkai High School,

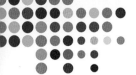

WELCOME TO Q:Skills for Success

Q: Skills for Success is a six-level series with two strands,
Reading and Writing **and** *Listening and Speaking***.**

READING AND WRITING

LISTENING AND SPEAKING

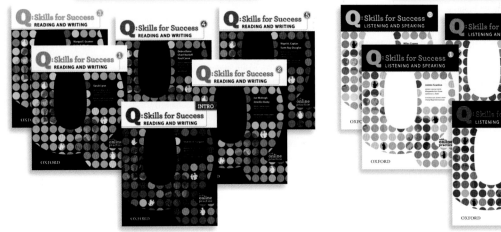

WITH Q ONLINE PRACTICE

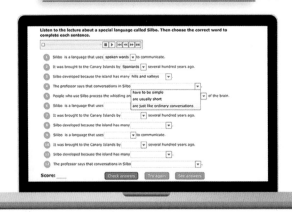

STUDENT AND TEACHER INFORMED

Q: Skills for Success is the result of an extensive development process involving thousands of teachers and hundreds of students around the world. Their views and opinions helped shape the content of the series. *Q* is grounded in teaching theory as well as real-world classroom practice, making it the most learner-centered series available.

CONTENTS

Q connects critical thinking, language skills, and learning outcomes.

LANGUAGE SKILLS

Explicit skills instruction enables students to meet their academic and professional goals.

LEARNING OUTCOMES

Clearly identified **learning outcomes** focus students on the goal of their instruction.

UNIT 3

Education

LISTENING	listening for examples
VOCABULARY	using the dictionary: antonyms
GRAMMAR	adjectives; adverbs + adjectives
PRONUNCIATION	sentence stress
SPEAKING	giving opinions

LEARNING OUTCOME

Share your opinions to plan a perfect school and present your plan to the class.

Unit QUESTION

What makes a good school?

PREVIEW THE UNIT

A Answer the questions about your school. Then compare with a partner.

1. How many students go to your school? _____
2. How many students are in your class? _____
3. What are two clubs at your school? _____
_____
4. What are two sports teams at your school? _____
_____

B Look at the photo. Where are the students? What are they doing?

C Discuss the Unit Question above with your classmates.

Listen to *The Q Classroom*, Track 21 on CD 1, to hear other answers.

32   UNIT 3

33

CRITICAL THINKING

Thought-provoking **unit questions** engage students with the topic and provide a **critical thinking framework** for the unit.

 Having the learning outcome is important because it gives students and teachers a clear idea of what the point of each task/activity in the unit is.
Lawrence Lawson, Palomar College, California

PREVIEW THE LISTENING

LANGUAGE SKILLS

Listening texts provide input on the unit question and give **exposure to academic content**.

Let's Take a Tour

A. You are going to listen to Sarah Carter, a student, give a tour of Watson University. Look at the map. Then match the names of the places with the definitions.

Watson University

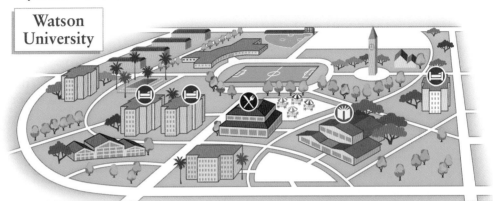

CRITICAL THINKING

Students **discuss** their opinions of each listening text and **analyze** how it changes their perspective on the unit question.

Q WHAT DO YOU THINK?

A. Give your opinion of the following statements. Circle *Yes* or *No*.

WATSON UNIVERSITY

What makes a good school?

1. Yes   No   It's important to learn a foreign language in school.
2. Yes   No   It's important to have good friends at school.
3. Yes   No   Every school needs a lot of clubs and teams.
4. Yes   No   A good school has computers for students to use.

> One of the best features is your focus on developing materials of a high "interest level."
> *Troy Hammond, Tokyo Gakugei University,*
> *International Secondary School, Japan*

Explicit skills instruction prepares students for academic success.

| Speaking Skill | Giving opinions | web+ |

CD 1
Track 25

Use the phrases *I think that . . .* and *In my opinion, . . .* to give an opinion.

☐ **I think that** students need computers.
☐ **In my opinion,** small classes are important.

You can answer opinions with *I agree* or *I disagree* followed by your opinion.

☐ A: **I think that** our school is great.
☐ B: **I agree.** I think that the classes are interesting.
☐ C: **I disagree.** In my opinion, the classes are too big.

CD 1
Track 26

A. Listen and complete the conversations. Use expressions from the box above. Compare answers with a partner.

1. A: _____ a good school gives a lot of tests. Then students study every day.

   B: _____. Class discussions make students study.

2. A: _____ sports are really important. Students need healthy bodies.

   B: _____. Exercise is very important.

3. A: _____ the food in our dining commons isn't very good. I don't like it!

   B: _____. _____ it tastes terrible. I usually cook my own food.

4. A: _____ we need a new library. The building is really old.

   B: _____. I like our library. _____ it's beautiful.

Tip for Success

When you write *In my opinion,* use a comma. Don't use a comma after *I think that.*

| Pronunciation | Sentence stress | web+ |

When you speak, you **stress** certain **important words**. This means you say them more loudly.

• Important words—like nouns, adjectives, and adverbs—give the information in the sentences.
• You do not usually stress words like pronouns, prepositions, *a/an/the,* the verb *be,* or the verb *do.*

CD 1
Track 23

☐ There are **two sports fields.**
   The **museum** is not **interesting.**
   We **go** to **school** in a **really dangerous neighborhood.**
   Do you **have** a **class today?**

CD 1
Track 24

A. Underline the stressed words. Listen and check your answers. Then practice the sentences with a partner.

lacrosse team

1. Does the school have a lacrosse team?
2. I have two classes in the morning.
3. We want a safe and clean school.
4. The college is in a dangerous city.
5. The coffee shops have free Internet access.
6. What is a good school?
7. Our sports field is pretty big.
8. My school is really great!
9. The buses to his school are very slow.
10. When does the class begin?

B. In your notebook, write five sentences about your school. Use adjectives and the adverbs *pretty, really, very,* and *extremely.*

C. Trade papers with a partner. Underline the stressed words. Then practice the sentences.

The <u>campus</u> is <u>extremely</u> <u>large</u>.

“ The tasks are simple, accessible, user-friendly, and very useful. ”
Jessica March, American University of Sharjah, U.A.E.

Tip for Success

Learning antonyms is a good way to build your vocabulary quickly. When you learn a new adjective, try to find out what its antonym is. Learners' dictionaries often give useful synonyms and antonyms.

Antonyms are words with opposite meanings. For example, *good* and *bad* are antonyms. Most forms of words—nouns, verbs, adjectives, adverbs, and prepositions—can have antonyms.

The dictionary often gives antonyms in the definition of a word. In the example below, notice the antonym of *hard*.

> **hard¹** /hard/ *adjective* (hard·er, hard·est)
> **1** not soft: *These apples are very hard.* • *I couldn't sleep because the bed was too hard.* ⊃ ANTONYM **soft**
> **2** difficult to do or understand: *The exam was very hard.* • *hard work* ⊃ ANTONYM **easy**
> **3** full of problems: *He's had **a hard life**.* ⊃ ANTONYM **easy**
> **4** not kind or gentle: *She is very **hard on** her children.* ⊃ ANTONYM **soft**

All dictionary entries are taken from the *Oxford Basic American Dictionary for learners of English* © Oxford University Press 2011.

All dictionary entries are taken from the *Oxford Basic American Dictionary for learners of English*.

LANGUAGE SKILLS

A **research-based vocabulary program** focuses students on the words they need to know academically and professionally, using skill strategies based on the same research as the Oxford dictionaries.

The ***Oxford Basic American Dictionary for learners of English*** was designed with English learners in mind, and provides extra learning tools for pronunciation, verb types, basic grammar structures, and more.

The Oxford 2000 Keywords 🔑
The Oxford 2000 keywords encompasses **the 2000 most important words to learn in English**. It is based on a comprehensive analysis of the Oxford English Corpus, a two-billion-word collection of English text, and on extensive research with both language and pedagogical experts.

The Academic Word List AWL
The Academic Word List was created by Averil Coxhead and contains **570 words that are commonly used in academic English**, such as in textbooks or articles across a wide range of academic subject areas. These words are a great place to start if you are studying English for academic purposes.

Clear learning outcomes focus students on the goals of instruction.

Unit Assignment | **Plan a perfect school**

 In this assignment, you plan a perfect school and present your plan to your class. This can be a high school, university, or other kind of school. As you prepare, think about the Unit Question, "What makes a good school?" and use the Self-Assessment checklist on page 44.

CONSIDER THE IDEAS

CD 1 Track 27

Listen to a group present their ideas for a perfect school. Check (✓) the ideas that they give. Then compare answers with a partner.

- ☐ 1. The perfect school is large.
- ☐ 2. The classes are very small.
- ☐ 3. The school has a lot of clubs, like a movie club and a soccer club.
- ☐ 4. There is a big gym.
- ☐ 5. Students get free computers.
- ☐ 6. The school is in a big city.
- ☐ 7. Apartments in town are cheap and beautiful.
- ☐ 8. Food on campus is cheap.

Check (✓) the skills you learned. If you need more work on a skill, refer to the page(s) in parentheses.

LISTENING	I can listen for examples. (p. 36)
VOCABULARY	I can use the dictionary to understand antonyms. (p. 37)
GRAMMAR	I can use adjectives and adverbs + adjectives. (p. 39)
PRONUNCIATION	I can use correct sentence stress. (p. 41)
SPEAKING	I can give my opinion. (p. 42)
LEARNING OUTCOME	I can share my opinions to plan a perfect school and present the plan to the class. (p. 43)

 Students can check their learning ... and they can focus on the essential points when they study.

Suh Yoomi, Seoul, South Korea

Q Online Practice

For the student

- **Easy-to-use:** a simple interface allows students to focus on enhancing their speaking and listening skills, not learning a new software program
- **Flexible:** for use anywhere there's an Internet connection
- **Access code card:** a *Q Online Practice* access code is included with this book—use the access code to register for *Q Online Practice* at www.Qonlinepractice.com

For the teacher

- **Simple yet powerful:** automatically grades student exercises and tracks progress
- **Straightforward:** online management system to review, print, or export reports
- **Flexible:** for use in the classroom or easily assigned as homework
- **Access code card:** with the *Q Teacher's Handbook* or sold separately

Teacher Resources

Q Teacher's Handbook gives strategic support through:

- specific teaching notes for each activity
- ideas for ensuring student participation
- multilevel strategies and expansion activities
- the answer key
- special sections on 21st century skills and critical thinking
- a **Testing Program CD-ROM** with a customizable test for each unit
- a **Q Online Practice** teacher's access code card

For additional resources visit the
Q: Skills for Success companion website at
www.oup.com/elt/teacher/Qskillsforsuccess

Q Class Audio includes:

- listening texts
- skills presentations and exercises
- *The Q Classroom*

 It's an interesting, engaging series which provides plenty of materials that are easy to use in class, as well as instructionally promising.
Donald Weasenforth, Collin College, Texas

UNIT	LISTENING	SPEAKING	VOCABULARY
1 **People** **Q** **What are you interested in?** LISTENING: Are You Interested in Art? Conversations (Greetings and Introductions)	• Identify information in an introduction • Predict content • Listen for main ideas • Listen for details	• Keep a conversation going by adding information • Keep a conversation going by showing you are thinking • Survey classmates about interests • Take notes to prepare for a presentation or discussion • Introduce a classmate	• Use collocations for hobbies and interests • Match definitions • Define new terms • Learn selected vocabulary words from the Oxford 2000 keywords and the Academic Word List
2 **Friendship** **Q** **How do you make friends?** LISTENING: Making Friends A Radio Program (Social Psychology)	• Listen for examples • Predict content • Listen for main ideas • Listen for details	• Ask and answer questions • Take notes to prepare for a presentation or discussion • Give a presentation on ways to make friends • Add more information to a presentation	• Use word categories to expand vocabulary • Match definitions • Define new terms • Learn selected vocabulary words from the Oxford 2000 keywords and the Academic Word List
3 **Education** **Q** **What makes a good school?** LISTENING: Let's Take a Tour A Campus Tour (Education)	• Predict content • Listen for main ideas • Listen for details • Listen for examples	• Give opinions • Express agreement and disagreement • Support ideas with examples and details • Take notes to prepare for a presentation or discussion • Present ideas to the class	• Use the dictionary to find antonyms and expand vocabulary • Match definitions • Define new terms • Learn selected vocabulary words from the Oxford 2000 keywords and the Academic Word List
4 **Food** **Q** **How do you choose your food?** LISTENING: Lifestyles and Food Choices A Radio Interview (Food and Nutrition)	• Listen for reasons • Predict content • Listen for main ideas • Listen for details	• Take notes to prepare for a presentation or discussion • Interview a classmate about food choices • Give opinions • Discuss results with the class	• Use prefixes and suffixes • Match definitions • Define new terms • Learn selected vocabulary words from the Oxford 2000 keywords and the Academic Word List

GRAMMAR	PRONUNCIATION	CRITICAL THINKING	UNIT OUTCOME
• Present of *be*; Simple present affirmative statements	• Simple present third-person *-s/-es*	• Identify sounds to demonstrate knowledge • Apply knowledge to complete a new task • Reflect on the unit question • Connect ideas and integrate information from multiple sources • Express ideas/reactions/opinions orally • Apply unit tips and use *Q Online Practice* to become a strategic learner	• Interview a classmate about his or her interests and introduce him or her to the class.
• Simple present	• Sentence intonation	• Define terms to demonstrate knowledge • Classify information to understand how things are similar and different • Apply knowledge to complete a new task • Reflect on the unit question • Connect ideas and integrate information from multiple sources • Express ideas/reactions/opinions orally • Apply unit tips and use *Q Online Practice* to become a strategic learner	• Give a presentation that describes some good ways to make friends, including details and examples.
• Adjectives; Adverbs + adjectives	• Sentence stress	• Discuss ideas to show understanding • Apply knowledge to complete a new task • Reflect on the unit question • Connect ideas and integrate information from multiple sources • Express ideas/reactions/opinions orally • Apply unit tips and use *Q Online Practice* to become a strategic learner	• Share your opinions to plan a perfect school and present your plan to the class.
• Verbs + gerunds and infinitives	• Stressed syllables	• Summarize information • Relate information to own experience • Reflect on the unit question • Connect ideas/integrate information from multiple sources • Express ideas/reactions/opinions orally • Apply unit tips and use *Q Online Practice* to become a strategic learner	• Design a survey about food and interview a classmate about his or her food choices.

UNIT	LISTENING	SPEAKING	VOCABULARY
5 Fun **What makes something fun?** **LISTENING:** Why Do You Come to the Park? A Report (Travel)	• Predict content • Listen for main ideas • Listen for details • Listen for reasons	• Agree with positive and negative opinions • Disagree politely • Discuss fun activities • Take notes to prepare for a presentation or discussion • Participate in a group discussion	• Use collocations with *do*, *play*, and *go* • Match definitions • Define new terms • Learn selected vocabulary words from the Oxford 2000 keywords and the Academic Word List
6 Home **What makes a good home?** **LISTENING 1:** How Do You Like Your Home? An Informal Survey (Sociology) **LISTENING 2:** Housing Problems, Housing Solutions A City Meeting (Urban Planning)	• Listen for opinions • Predict content • Listen for main ideas • Listen for details	• Discuss ideas • Take notes to prepare for a presentation or discussion • Agree and disagree • Give a presentation	• Use compound nouns • Match definitions • Define new terms • Learn selected vocabulary words from the Oxford 2000 keywords and the Academic Word List
7 Weather **How does the weather affect you?** **LISTENING 1:** The World of Weather A Weather Report (News and Weather) **LISTENING 2:** Weather and Our Moods A Lecture (Psychology)	• Predict content • Listen for main ideas • Listen for details • Listen for opinions	• Ask for repetition • Ask and answer questions • Take notes to prepare for a presentation or discussion • Participate in a group discussion	• Use nouns and adjectives for weather • Match definitions • Define new terms • Learn selected vocabulary words from the Oxford 2000 keywords and the Academic Word List
8 Health **What do you do to stay healthy?** **LISTENING 1:** Health Watch A Podcast Interview (Health and Wellness) **LISTENING 2:** How Often Do You Work Out? An Interview (Behavior and Health)	• Listen for frequency • Predict content • Listen for main ideas • Listen for details	• Describe problems • Give advice • Take notes to prepare for a presentation or discussion • Conduct a survey • Ask for repetition • Discuss results	• Use adjectives ending in *-ed* • Match definitions • Define new terms • Learn selected vocabulary words from the Oxford 2000 keywords and the Academic Word List

GRAMMAR	PRONUNCIATION	CRITICAL THINKING	UNIT OUTCOME
• Subject and object pronouns	• Reduced pronouns	• Practice to apply information to new situations • Support ideas with reasons • Reflect on the unit question • Connect ideas/integrate information from multiple sources • Express ideas/reactions/opinions orally • Apply unit tips and use *Q Online Practice* to become a strategic learner	• Participate in a group discussion about fun places in your area.
• Prepositions of location	• Stress in compound nouns	• Identify pros and cons • Rank items and make evaluations • Apply knowledge to complete a new task • Reflect on the unit question • Connect ideas/integrate information from multiple sources • Express ideas/reactions/opinions orally • Apply unit tips and use *Q Online Practice* to become a strategic learner	• Design your perfect home and present your design to the class.
• Adverbs of frequency	• Stressing important words	• Use a chart to organize information • Apply information to personal experience • Reflect on the unit question • Connect ideas/integrate information from multiple sources • Express ideas/reactions/opinions orally • Apply unit tips and use *Q Online Practice* to become a strategic learner	• Participate in a group discussion about weather.
• Modals *can* and *should*	• *can, can't, should,* and *shouldn't*	• Relate ideas to own experience • Compare and contrast habits to understand ideas more deeply • Reflect on the unit question • Connect ideas/integrate information from multiple sources • Express ideas/reactions/opinions orally • Apply unit tips and use *Q Online Practice* to become a strategic learner	• Create, conduct, and discuss a health survey.

UNIT	LISTENING	SPEAKING	VOCABULARY
9 Cities **Q** **What makes a city special?** **LISTENING 1:** Travel Talk A Radio Program (Geography and Travel) **LISTENING 2:** Making Positive Changes A Speech (Government and Economics)	• Predict content • Listen for main ideas • Listen for details • Listen for frequency	• Use open questions • Participate in a discussion • Take notes to prepare for a presentation or discussion • Give a presentation	• Use the dictionary to understand word families and expand vocabulary • Match definitions • Define new terms • Learn selected vocabulary words from the Oxford 2000 keywords and the Academic Word List
10 Milestones **Q** **What are the most important events in someone's life?** **LISTENING 1:** Ania Filochowska: A Young Genius A Radio Quiz (Biography) **LISTENING 2:** Naguib Mahfouz: A Successful Writer A Class Presentation (Literature)	• Listen for sequence • Listen for numbers • Predict content • Listen for main ideas • Listen for details	• Take notes to prepare for a presentation or discussion • Interview a classmate • Use open questions • Give a presentation to the class	• Use phrases with *get* • Match definitions • Define new terms • Learn selected vocabulary words from the Oxford 2000 keywords and the Academic Word List

GRAMMAR	PRONUNCIATION	CRITICAL THINKING	UNIT OUTCOME
• Past of *be*; Simple past affirmative statements	• *-ed* endings	• Combine information from different sources to come up with new ideas • Discuss problems and solutions • Reflect on the unit question • Connect ideas/integrate information from multiple sources • Express ideas/reactions/ opinions orally • Apply unit tips and use *Q Online Practice* to become a strategic learner	• Give a presentation about a special city using the simple present and simple past.
• Simple past with regular and irregular verbs	• Numbers with *-teen* and *-ty*	• Choose most important milestones • Apply knowledge to complete a new task • Reflect on the unit question • Connect ideas/integrate information from multiple sources • Express ideas/reactions/ opinions orally • Apply unit tips and use *Q Online Practice* to become a strategic learner	• Interview a classmate about the most important events in his or her life and present them to the class.

UNIT 1

People

VOCABULARY ●	collocations for hobbies and interests
GRAMMAR ●	present of *be*; simple present affirmative statements
PRONUNCIATION ●	simple present third-person *-s/-es*
SPEAKING ●	keeping a conversation going

LEARNING OUTCOME ●

Interview a classmate about his or her interests and introduce him or her to the class.

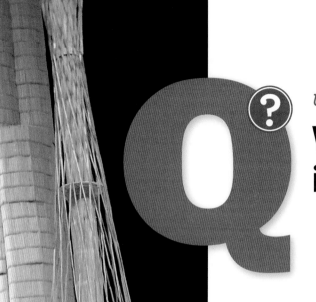

?

Unit QUESTION

What are you interested in?

PREVIEW THE UNIT

A What do you talk about with a new friend? Circle the topics.

your favorite movie	your favorite music	your job
your age	your family	your weight
your favorite sports	your name	your hometown

B Look at the photo. What is the man doing?

C Discuss the Unit Question above with your classmates.

Listen to *The Q Classroom*, Track 2 on CD 1, to hear other answers.

LISTENING | Are You Interested in Art?

VOCABULARY

A. Here are some words from the Listening. Read the definitions. Then circle the correct word to complete each conversation.

> **belong to** (*verb*) to be a member of a group
>
> **club** (*noun*) a group of people—they meet and do things together
>
> **collect** (*verb*) to get and keep many things because you like them
>
> **good at** (*phrase*) can do something well
>
> **hobbies** (*noun*) activities—you do them for fun
>
> **instrument** (*noun*) something you use to play music
>
> **interested in** (*phrase*) enjoying an activity or a topic
>
> **team** (*noun*) a group of people—they play a sport or a game together

chess

1. A: Do you (collect / belong to) the chess club?

   B: Yes, I do. We meet on Thursdays.

2. A: I like basketball, but I can't play it well.

   B: My roommate is very (good at / team) basketball. He can teach you.

3. A: Do you play a(n) (instrument / team)?

   B: Yes, I do. I play the piano.

4. A: Wow, you're a great soccer player! Are you on the soccer (hobbies / team)?

   B: Thanks! Yes, I am.

5. A: What do you like to do?

   B: Oh, I have a lot of (interested in / hobbies). I play the guitar, I go hiking, and I like old movies.

6. A: Is there a movie (team / club) at this school?

   B: Yes, there is. We meet at the movie theater every Wednesday night. It's fun!

7. A: You have a lot of postcards!

   B: I (hobbies / collect) them. I have over 2,000 postcards from all over the world.

8. A: I like the museum. Are you (belong to / interested in) art?

   B: Yes. I'm not good at art, but I like it.

B. Read the sentences. Circle *T* (true) or *F* (false). For false answers, write a new sentence with true information. Then compare answers with a partner.

1. T F I collect coins. _____

2. T F I belong to a book club. _____

3. T F I am interested in sports. _____

4. T F I am good at art. _____

5. T F My hobbies are soccer and cooking. _____

PREVIEW THE LISTENING

| **Are You Interested in Art?**

You are going to listen to three conversations at a school. Look at the pictures. Match each question with the correct picture.

1. ____   2. ____   3. ____

a. Can I sit here?

b. Is that a good book?

c. Is this Professor Kim's music history class?

COMPREHENSION CHECK

CD 1
Track 3
A. Read the sentences. Then listen to all three conversations. Write *T* (true) or *F* (false) for each sentence.

_____ a. All the speakers are students.

_____ b. All the speakers have hobbies.

_____ c. All the speakers know each other well.

CD 1
Track 3
B. Listen again. What are the people interested in? Check (✓) the correct activities. (You will not check all the activities.)

1. Lin	☐ video games	☐ hiking	☐ movies	☐ art
James	☐ video games	☐ hiking	☐ movies	☐ art
2. David	☐ books	☐ chess	☐ comic books	☐ soccer
Anna	☐ books	☐ chess	☐ comic books	☐ soccer
3. Sam	☐ guitar	☐ piano	☐ soccer	☐ tennis
Mika	☐ guitar	☐ piano	☐ soccer	☐ tennis

CD 1
Track 3
C. Read the sentences. Then listen again. Circle the correct answers.

1. a. Lin goes hiking with her friends every

   (Thursday / weekend / afternoon).

   b. James belongs to the (movie / art / hiking) club.

2. a. Anna's book club reads (one / ten / twelve) books a year.

   b. David is on the (tennis / soccer / baseball) team.

3. a. Sam's father plays the (piano / guitar / drums).

   b. Mika's favorite sport is (tennis / soccer / baseball).

Some words usually go together. These are called **collocations**.

Verb + preposition + noun	Verb + noun
be good at volleyball / the piano	**go** shopping / hiking
be interested in movies / sports / art	**play** sports / chess / the guitar / games
be on a team	**read** books / magazines
belong to a book club	**ride** a bicycle / a bike
get together with friends	**see** a movie
go to a museum / the beach / a park	**take** lessons
listen to music	**watch** a DVD / television
live in Tokyo	

CD 1
Track 4

A. Complete the collocations with words from the box above. Then listen to check your answers.

Liz Alan lives _____ 1 Toronto. She works at the after-school program at the community center in her town. Children come to the community center after school. Liz does many activities with them. It's a good job for her because she is interested _____ 2 a lot of different things. She is good _____ 3 sports. She also likes music and she can _____ 4 the guitar. She sings songs with the kids. The kids can also _____ 5 piano and guitar lessons. On sunny days, Liz and the kids _____ 6 bikes or _____ 7 hiking. Sometimes they go _____ 8 the beach or the park. On rainy days, Liz and the kids _____ 9 DVDs, or they _____ 10 games like chess and checkers. Sometimes they _____ 11 to a museum together. After work, Liz sometimes gets _____ 12 with friends, but she usually goes home to relax and _____ 13 a book.

B. Listen to the people talk about themselves. Write two sentences about each speaker. Use the words in parentheses.

1. **Sun-Hee** (reads) _____

   (is interested in) _____

2. **Khalid** (plays) _____

   (rides) _____

C. In your notebook, write five sentences about you. Use collocations from the Building Vocabulary box on page 7.

WHAT DO YOU THINK?

A. Go around the class. Ask these questions. When someone answers *yes*, write down his or her name. Try to write a different name for each question.

A: Do you belong to a club?

B: Yes, I do. I belong to a soccer club.

Question	Name
1. Do you belong to a club?	
2. Are you interested in movies?	
3. Do you play the guitar?	
4. Are you good at chess?	
5. Are you on a sports team?	
6. Do you ride a bicycle to class?	
7. Do you get together with friends on Saturdays?	
8. Do you take any lessons?	

 for Success

Use the word *too* to add information. It has the same meaning as *also*.

B. Share your answers in groups.

A: Eric belongs to a soccer club.

B: Susan belongs to a soccer club, too.

Present of *be*

Use the verb *be* to identify and describe people and things.

Tip for Success

Statements with *be* are followed by nouns (*a student*), adjectives (*tired*), or prepositional phrases (*from China*).

Affirmative and negative statements				Contractions			
subject	be	(not)		subject + be	(not)	subject	be + not
I	am		a student.	I'm			
You We They	are	(not)	tired.	You're We're They're	(not)	You We They	aren't.
He She It	is		from China.	He's She's It's		He She It	isn't.

- A **contraction** makes two words into one word. It has an apostrophe (').
- You usually use contractions in speaking.
- There are two negative contractions for *are not* and *is not*.
  are not = 're not/aren't   is not = 's not/isn't

Yes/No questions			Short answers	
be	subject		yes	no
Are	you		Yes, I **am**.	No, I'm **not**.
Is	he	interested in cooking?	Yes, he **is**.	No, he's **not**. No, he **isn't**.
Are	they		Yes, they **are**.	No, they're **not**. No, they **aren't**.

- In questions, the verb *be* comes before the subject.
- You can also answer *yes/no* questions with just *yes* or *no*.

Information questions				Answers	
wh- word	*be*	subject			
How old	**are**	you?		18.	I'm 18 years old.
What	**is**	she	interested in?	Music.	She's interested in music.
Where	**are**	they	from?	Chile.	They're from Chile.

- Answer an information question with a short answer or a complete sentence. You often use short answers in conversation.

Simple present

The simple present describes habits, facts, or feelings.

> He **plays** soccer on Saturdays.
> They **live** in Japan.
> I **feel** tired.

Affirmative Statements		
subject	verb	
I - You - We - They	**come**	from Canada.
He - She – It	**comes**	

- Use the verb + *-s* or *-es* after *he*, *she*, and *it*. For spelling rules, see page 182.

A. Put the words in the correct order. Then take turns asking and answering the questions with a partner. Write your partner's answers. Use complete sentences.

1. you / from / where / are <u>Where are you from</u> ?

   Partner's answer: _____

2. interested / art / you / in / are _____ ?

   Partner's answer: _____

3. at / you / are / what / good _____ ?

   Partner's answer: _____

4. years / 20 / old / you / are _____ ?

   Partner's answer: _____

5. on / you / are / a team _____?

Partner's answer: _____

B. Complete the conversations with the correct forms of the verbs in the box. (You will use some words more than once. Some forms will be negative.) Then practice with a partner.

be	belong	go	like	listen	live	play	take

hiking

1. **Toshi:** Mika, what _____ you interested in?

   Mary: Well, I _____ hiking on the weekends. And on

   Fridays, I _____ French lessons.

2. **Emma:** _____ your friend interested in sports?

   Mika: Yes, she _____. She _____ to a

   soccer club.

3. **Sam:** _____ your parents from China?

   Sarah: No, they _____. They _____ from

   Korea, but they _____ in the United States now.

4. **Sun-Hee:** _____ you good at chess? I _____

   chess a lot.

   Rob: No, I _____ good at chess. But my father

   _____ chess often. And my brothers

   _____ to a chess club.

5. **Carlos:** _____ your friends interested in hiking?

   Matt: Yes, they _____. They _____ hiking

   every weekend.

6. **Kate:** Is Tom interested in music?

   John: Yes, he _____. He _____ to jazz and

   classical music a lot, but his favorite is pop.

CD 1
Track 6

There are three ways to pronounce the final -s or -es of a simple present verb.

/ s /	/ z /	/ ɪz /
gets makes	listens plays	watch**es** wash**es**

CD 1
Track 7

A. Listen to the sentences. Circle the sound that you hear at the end of the verb. Then practice the sentences with a partner.

Tip **Critical Thinking**

Activity A asks you to **identify** the sound you hear. This is one way to show you understand the lesson.

1. He goes shopping on Saturdays.   / s /   / z /   / ɪz /

2. Khalid works downtown.   / s /   / z /   / ɪz /

3. Sam plays video games in the evening.   / s /   / z /   / ɪz /

4. Sun-Hee sometimes watches TV after work.   / s /   / z /   / ɪz /

5. Mary gets together with friends on Sundays.   / s /   / z /   / ɪz /

6. Mika lives in Los Angeles.   / s /   / z /   / ɪz /

7. David washes his car on Saturdays.   / s /   / z /   / ɪz /

8. Emma belongs to a golf club.   / s /   / z /   / ɪz /

B. Write five sentences about friends. Use the verbs in the box.

belongs   gets   goes   plays   takes   washes   watches

1. _____

2. _____

3. _____

4. _____

5. _____

C. Read your sentences from Activity B to a partner. For each of your partner's sentences, circle the sound you hear in the chart.

1. / s /   / z /   / ɪz /   **3.** / s /   / z /   / ɪz /   **5.** / s /   / z /   / ɪz /
2. / s /   / z /   / ɪz /   **4.** / s /   / z /   / ɪz /

Adding information

Short answers to questions do not help conversations. Give extra information to keep your conversation going.

 CD 1
Track 8

Answer is too short	Answer is good
A: Rome is my favorite city. What's yours? B: Bangkok.	A: Rome is my favorite city. What's yours? B: **Bangkok. It has amazing buildings and delicious food!**
A: I like cooking. How about you? B: **I like cooking, too.**	A: I like cooking. How about you? B: **I like cooking, too. I often cook with friends on the weekends.**

Tip for Success

Ask short questions like *How about you?* or *What's yours?* to get the other person's opinion or answer.

Write answers to the questions. Add extra information. Then ask and answer the questions with a partner.

1. A: What are your hobbies?

   B: _____

2. A: I like soccer. How about you?

   B: _____

3. A: What are you good at?

   B: _____

4. A: *Avatar* is my favorite movie. What's yours?

   B: _____

5. A: Are you interested in art?

   B: _____

6. A: I'm interested in cooking. How about you?

   B: _____

Avatar

Taking time to think

Sometimes you can't answer a question right away. Use these special
expressions before you answer. They tell people, "I am thinking."

CD 1
Track 9

Hmm.   Let's see.   Let me see.   Let me think.   Uh.   Well.

CD 1
Track 10

**A. Listen to the conversation. Write expressions from the box above.
Then practice the conversation with a partner.**

Tom: Carlos, what's your favorite sport?

Carlos: _____, it's soccer. But I also like basketball.
          1
What's yours?

Tom: _____. It's probably volleyball. I play on the beach in
        2
the summer.

Carlos: Where's your favorite beach?

Tom: _____. Miami has a really good beach.
        3

Carlos: _____, what's your favorite beach near here?
          4

Tom: Ocean Beach is my favorite. It's beautiful! Do you know any beaches

near here?

Carlos: _____. _____, I like East Beach. It has
          5   6
really big waves. People surf there.

**B. Work with a partner. Practice the questions and answers in the
Activity on page 13 again. Take time to think when you answer. Use
special expressions like *Hmm* and *Let me think*.**

A: What are your hobbies?
B: Let me think. I like games. I play chess a lot.

In this assignment, you will interview a classmate about his or her interests and introduce him or her to the class. As you prepare, think about the Unit Question, "What are you interested in?" and use the Self-Assessment checklist on page 16.

CONSIDER THE IDEAS

A. What do you say in an introduction? Check (✓) the information.

☐ a greeting   ☐ weight
☐ age   ☐ favorite movie
☐ telephone number   ☐ hobbies and interests
☐ country   ☐ name
☐ job   ☐ family problems

CD 1
Track 11

B. Listen to this sample introduction. Then look at the list in Activity A. What information is in the introduction? Circle the ideas in Activity A.

> Good afternoon. This is my friend Ivan. Ivan is from Russia. He's a computer engineer. Ivan is interested in hiking in the mountains. He goes hiking once a month. Ivan is good at soccer. He belongs to a soccer club and plays every weekend. Ivan also plays the piano. He gets together with his friends to play classical music. Ivan sees a lot of movies. His favorite movie is *Avatar*.

PREPARE AND SPEAK

A. GATHER IDEAS Work with a partner. Follow these steps.

1. Add a question to the list on page 16.

2. Use the questions to interview a partner. Write down your partner's answers in the questionnaire.

3. When you answer the questions, give extra information (not just short answers). Use special expressions like *Hmm* and *Let me think*.

Personal Questionnaire

1. What's your name?

2. Where are you from?

3. What's your favorite movie?

4. What's your favorite food?

5. What are your hobbies and interests?

6. What are you good at?

7.

B. **ORGANIZE IDEAS** In your notebook, write 5–6 interesting sentences about your partner. Use the information from Activity A.

C. **SPEAK** Use your sentences to introduce your partner to the class. Include a greeting like "Good morning" and the introduction phrase "This is . . . " Look at the Self-Assessment checklist below before you begin.

CHECK AND REFLECT

A. **CHECK** Think about the Unit Assignment and complete the Self-Assessment checklist.

SELF-ASSESSMENT		
Yes	No	
☐	☐	My introduction was clear.
☐	☐	I used vocabulary from this unit.
☐	☐	I used the verb be and simple present statements correctly.
☐	☐	I included interesting information about my partner.

B. **REFLECT** Discuss these questions with a partner.

1. What is something new you learned in this unit?

2. Think about the Unit Question, "What are you interested in?" What are three things you are interested in?

Track Your Success

Circle the words you learned in this unit.

Nouns
club 🔑
cooking 🔑
hobby
instrument 🔑
team 🔑 AWL

Verbs
belong (to) 🔑
collect 🔑

Phrases
good at
interested in

Collocations
be good at volleyball /
   the piano
be interested in movies /
   sports / art
be on a team
belong to a book club
get together with friends
go to a museum /
   the beach / a park
listen to music

live in Tokyo
go shopping / hiking
play sports / chess /
   the guitar / games
read books / magazines
ride a bicycle / a bike
see a movie
take lessons
watch a DVD / television

🔑 Oxford 2000 keywords
AWL Academic Word List
For more information on the Oxford 2000 keywords and AWL, see page xi.

Check (✓) the skills you learned. If you need more work on a skill, refer to the page(s) in parentheses.

VOCABULARY	●	I can understand collocations for hobbies and interests. (p. 7)
GRAMMAR	●	I can use the present of *be* and simple present affirmative statements. (p. 9)
PRONUNCIATION	●	I can pronounce simple present third-person *-s/-es*. (p. 12)
SPEAKING	●	I can keep a conversation going. (pp. 13–14)
LEARNING OUTCOME	●	I can interview a classmate about his or her interests and introduce him or her to the class. (p. 15)

UNIT 2

Friendship

LISTENING ●	listening for examples
VOCABULARY ●	word categories
GRAMMAR ●	simple present
PRONUNCIATION ●	sentence intonation
SPEAKING ●	adding more information

LEARNING OUTCOME

Give a presentation that describes some good ways to make friends, including details and examples.

Unit QUESTION

How do you make friends?

PREVIEW THE UNIT

A Which activities are good for making friends? Check (✓) the activities. Then compare with a partner.

☐ get together with relatives
☐ watch television at home
☐ take an exercise class
☐ play basketball at a park
☐ go to a shopping mall
☐ go to events, like festivals

☐ read a book
☐ belong to a hiking club
☐ take piano lessons
☐ see a movie
☐ go online
☐ go to a museum

B Look at the photo. What are the people doing? Is this a good way to make friends?

C Discuss the Unit Question above with your classmates.

🔊 Listen to *The Q Classroom*, Track 12 on CD 1, to hear other answers.

LISTENING | Making Friends

Vocabulary

A. Here are some words from the Listening. Read the sentences. Which explanation is correct? Circle *a* or *b*.

1. Anna is smart and has many good ideas. Sometimes Mary has problems, so Anna gives Mary **advice**.
   a. Mary gives Anna ideas to help her.
   b. Anna gives Mary ideas to help her.

2. Rob doesn't like to see movies alone. He wants to **join** a movie club.
   a. Rob wants to become a part of a group and see movies.
   b. Rob wants to meet people at the movies.

3. Sarah and Emma **share** an interest in soccer. They both like tennis, too.
   a. Sarah likes soccer, but Emma likes tennis.
   b. Sarah and Emma are both interested in soccer.

4. Mika likes to help people. She is a **volunteer**. After she finishes work, she reads to the patients at a hospital.
   a. Mika gets money to read to people.
   b. Mika reads to people for free.

5. Toshi is very **positive**. He likes everyone and enjoys his life.
   a. Toshi thinks about good things in his life.
   b. Toshi thinks about bad things in his life.

6. John and James meet every day. They are **close** friends.
   a. John and James are good friends.
   b. John and James are new friends.

7. Matt always **smiles** at other people. People usually like Matt.
   a. Matt has an angry look on his face.
   b. Matt has a happy look on his face.

8. Isabel often gives **compliments** to her friends. She says things like, "I like your shoes."
   a. Isabel says nice things to people.
   b. Isabel isn't nice to other people.

B. Complete the sentences with the words from Activity A. (You will not use all the words.)

1. Students _____ many different clubs at my school.

2. Carlos always gives me nice _____. Today, he said, "You're a really good student."

3. Hassan and Khalid are _____ friends. They do everything together.

4. Karen is a _____. She gives food to people at a food bank.

5. Sun-Hee and Mika's biology class is difficult. They often _____ their class notes with each other.

6. Matt is never angry or sad. He's always _____.

a food bank

PREVIEW THE LISTENING

Making Friends

You are going to listen to three conversations on a radio program. Three people give advice about making friends. Look at the three photos. Match each name with a photo.

1. ___   2. ___   3. ___

a. David Scott, volunteer

b. Katie Jones, teacher

c. Dr. Mary Johnson, counselor

COMPREHENSION CHECK

A. Listen to the three conversations. Who gives each piece of advice?
Match the advice with the people.

People	Advice
1. Katie Jones	a. Be positive.
__f__	b. Smile and look at people.
2. David Scott	c. Give compliments and ask questions.
___ ___	d. Join a team or club.
3. Dr. Johnson	e. Be a volunteer.
___ ___	f. Don't stay at home.

B. Read the sentences. Listen again. Write *T* (true) or *F* (false) for each
statement. Then correct each false statement to make it true.

1. a. _F_ Katie teaches at a ~~high school~~. *college*

   b. ___ Katie belongs to a hiking club.

2. a. ___ David cleans up a beach on Saturdays.

   b. ___ David has lunch with friends on Saturdays.

3. a. ___ Dr. Johnson and Rob are close friends.

   b. ___ Dr. Johnson doesn't give advice for shy people.

Building Vocabulary   Word categories

A category is a group of similar things. Categories can help you learn
vocabulary. For example, when you learn the name of a musical instrument,
learn the names of three or four other instruments.

Musical instruments: flute, guitar, piano, violin

Sometimes you can use the expressions *is a kind of* and *is a type of* to explain a
word. You say the new word and give its category.

Football **is a kind of** sport.   Jazz **is a type of** music.

A. Complete the chart with words from the box. Some words can go in more than one category. Then add two words to each category. Use your dictionary to help you.

biology	chess	classical	cooking	French
history	math	reading	rock	skiing
Spanish	tennis	volleyball	video games	

Music	Hobbies	Classes	Sports

B. Listen to the four conversations. The speakers explain these words. Add them to the chart in Activity A.

1. chorus / folk
2. calculus / lacrosse
3. blues / rugby
4. racquetball / physics

C. Ask and answer these questions with a partner. Use your own ideas.

1. **A:** What's _____?
   B: It's a kind of music.

2. **A:** What's _____?
   B: It's a kind of food.

3. **A:** What's _____?
   B: It's a type of sport.

4. **A:** What's a(n) _____?
   B: It's a type of instrument.

CD 1 Track 15

People **give examples with *like*.** *Like* comes in the middle of a sentence.

☐ I meet new people in different places, **like** the library or the coffee shop.

People also **give examples with *for example*.** *For example* can come at the beginning of a sentence.

☐ Matt is always busy. **For example**, he takes Spanish lessons on Thursdays, he plays tennis on Saturdays, and he works five days a week.

CD 1 Track 16

A. **Listen to Kate and Sun-Hee's conversation. Complete the sentences.**

1. Sun-Hee belongs to the _____ club.

2. Sun-Hee is interested in languages. She loves _____ and

   _____.

3. Kate says Sun-Hee can talk about easy topics. She can talk about

   _____ and _____.

Sun-Hee and Kate

4. Sun-Hee can go to _____ or _____ with the

   girls from her class.

CD 1 Track 17

B. **Listen to parts of the conversation again. What do you hear—*for example* or *like*? Circle the correct answer.**

1. for example / like   3. for example / like

2. for example / like   4. for example / like

 WHAT DO YOU THINK?

A. **How do you make friends? Check (✓) the things you do. Add two ideas.**

☐ I am positive.   ☐ I meet people at work.

☐ I play sports.   ☐ I meet people in my classes.

☐ I belong to clubs.   ☐ _____

☐ I work as a volunteer.   ☐ _____

B. **Talk with a partner. Explain three things you do to make friends.**

A: How do you make friends?   *B: I play sports. I play tennis and lacrosse.*

Grammar | **Simple present**

The simple present describes habits, facts, and feelings.

Affirmative statements

subject	verb	
I - You - We - They	**play**	soccer.
He - She	**plays**	soccer.

- Use the base verb + -s or -es after *he*, *she*, and *it*.

Negative statements

subject	do/does + not	verb	
I - You - We - They	**do not** **don't**		soccer.
He - She	**does not** **doesn't**	**play**	soccer.

- Use *do* with *I*, *we*, *you*, and *they*.
- Use *does* with *he*, *she*, and *it*.

Yes/No questions				Short answers	
do/does	subject	verb		yes	no
Do	you we they	**like**	tennis?	Yes, I **do.** Yes, you **do.** Yes, they **do.**	No, I **don't.** No, you **don't.** No, they **don't.**
Does	he she			Yes, he **does.** Yes, she **does.**	No, he **doesn't.** No, she **doesn't.**

Tip for Success

Remember: You can also give a short answer to an information question.
A: Where do you live?
B: In Tokyo.

Information questions				Answers
wh- word	do/does	subject		
What	**do**	you	**do?**	I **teach** history.
Where	**do**	you	**live?**	I **live** in Tokyo.
When	**does**	he	**play** tennis?	He **plays** tennis on Saturdays.

A. Complete the conversations. Use the simple present form of the verbs and contractions. Then practice the conversations with a partner.

1. **A:** _____ (how often / you / see) James?

   B: I _____ (not / see) him every day, but we're close friends.

   A: _____ (he / play) basketball at the park with

   you on Saturdays?

   B: Yes, he _____ (do). We _____ (play)

   soccer together on Sundays, too.

2. **A:** I _____ (share) a lot of interests with my friends. For

   example, we all _____ (belong) to a hiking club.

   B: _____ (where / you / go) hiking?

   A: We _____ (go) to Mount Davidson. _____

   _____ (you / want) to come with us next week?

3. **A:** I _____ (like) your jacket.

   _____ (where / you / shop)?

   B: I _____ (buy) clothes at the mall. My favorite store is

   Cindy's. Their clothes _____ (not / cost) a lot of money.

   A: Oh, I _____ (love) that store. My friend Mika

   _____ (work) there.

B. Rewrite these incorrect sentences. Use contractions.

Do you like video games?

1. He don't know anyone here. _He doesn't know anyone here._____

2. What does the volunteers do? _____

3. Shy people don't talks a lot. _____

4. Do the class begin at 3:00? _____

5. Do you likes video games? _____

6. She don't listen to rock music. _____

C. Put the words in the correct order. Write one new question. Then ask and answer the questions with a partner. Give complete answers.

1. you / where / people / do / usually meet

   _____?

   Partner's answer: _____

2. know / do / on your street / people / you

   _____?

   Partner's answer: _____

3. your / do / what / you / do / with / friends

   _____?

   Partner's answer: _____

4. you / go / friends / where / with / your / do

   _____?

   Partner's answer: _____

5. New question: _____

   Partner's answer: _____

Pronunciation   Sentence intonation

Intonation is the rise ↑ or fall ↓ of your voice in sentences.

In **affirmative and negative statements**, your voice falls at the end.

CD 1
Track 18

I have a problem.　　　　He doesn't play sports.

Yes/No **questions**

In *yes/no* questions, your voice goes up at the end.

Do you belong to a club?　　　Does she live in China?

Information questions

In information questions, your voice goes down at the end.

What do you mean?　　　When does it start?

CD 1
Track 19

A. Circle *rising* or *falling* for each sentence. Listen and check your answers. Then practice the sentences.

1.	Does your brother play baseball?	rising	falling
2.	What classes do you have today?	rising	falling
3.	Do you have any advice?	rising	falling
4.	I don't know David.	rising	falling
5.	I'm in the book club.	rising	falling
6.	Do you like soccer?	rising	falling
7.	How about you?	rising	falling
8.	Sometimes I play basketball.	rising	falling
9.	Where does the tennis club meet?	rising	falling
10.	He doesn't make friends easily.	rising	falling

B. Practice the conversations in Grammar Activity A on page 26 with a partner. Pay attention to your intonation.

Unit Assignment | **Give a presentation about good ways to make friends**

In this assignment, you will give a presentation about good ways to make friends. As you prepare, think about the Unit Question, "How do you make friends?" and use the Self-Assessment checklist on page 30.

CONSIDER THE IDEAS

CD 1
Track 20

Listen to the presentation. The group talks about four ways to make friends. Write down one example for each category.

1. Become a volunteer: _____

2. Join a club: _____

3. Join a team: _____

4. Take a class: _____

PREPARE AND SPEAK

A. GATHER IDEAS Work in a group of four. Follow these steps.

Tip for Success

Examples make your ideas clearer. Use the expressions *like* and *for example* to give examples.

1. Discuss the question, "What are good ways to make friends in your city?" Use ideas from the box or your own ideas.

join a club	take a class	join a team	become a volunteer
go online	be positive	give compliments	

A: *What are good ways to make friends in this city?*
B: *Join a team. That's a good way to make friends.*
C: *What kind of teams do we have?*
D: *We have a lot of teams, like a soccer team and tennis team.*

2. Choose four ideas and write them in the chart below. Then write at least two examples for each way to make friends.

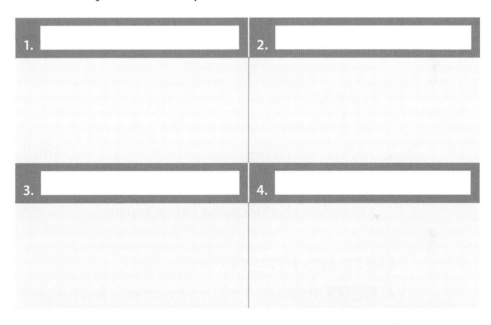

1.	2.
3.	4.

join a tennis team

take a cooking class

In your part of the presentation, remember to add extra information, like details and examples. This makes your presentation more interesting. Review the Speaking Skill box in Unit 1, page 13.

> I'm on the lacrosse team. Every Sunday, we play against teams from all over the city.

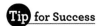

Tip for Success

Before a presentation, it's important to practice. Practice two or three times with your group.

B. **ORGANIZE IDEAS** Work with your group. Prepare your presentation.

1. Look at the chart in Activity A. Each group member chooses a category.

2. Write your part of the presentation.
   - Give at least one example for your category.
   - Add information about your example.

3. First Speaker: Use this sentence as your introduction.

   Good [morning, afternoon, evening]. We are presenting four good ways to make friends here in [your city's name].

4. Last Speaker: Use a sentence like this at the end.

   Thank you. Do you have any questions?

5. Practice your presentation.

C. **SPEAK** Present your information to your class. Look at the Self-Assessment checklist below before you begin.

CHECK AND REFLECT

A. **CHECK** Think about the Unit Assignment and complete the Self-Assessment checklist.

SELF-ASSESSMENT		
Yes	No	
☐	☐	My part of the presentation was clear.
☐	☐	I used vocabulary from this unit.
☐	☐	I used the simple present correctly.
☐	☐	I gave clear examples to help the audience understand.
☐	☐	I added information, like details and examples.

B. **REFLECT** **Discuss these questions with a partner.**

1. What is something new you learned in this unit?

2. Think about the Unit Question, "How do you make friends?" Do you use any of the ideas in the unit?

Track Your Success

Circle the words you learned in this unit.

Nouns
advice 🔑
biology
blues
calculus
chorus
classical AWL
compliment
flute
folk
football 🔑
French
guitar

history 🔑
jazz
lacrosse
math 🔑
piano
racquetball
reading
rock 🔑
rugby
skiing
Spanish
violin
volunteer AWL

Adjectives
close 🔑
positive 🔑

Phrases
be a kind of
be a type of

Verbs
join 🔑
share 🔑
smile 🔑

🔑 Oxford 2000 keywords
AWL Academic Word List

Check (✓) the skills you learned. If you need more work on a skill, refer to the page(s) in parentheses.

LISTENING	●	I can identify examples. (p. 24)
VOCABULARY	●	I can use categories to learn new words. (p. 22)
GRAMMAR	●	I can use the simple present. (p. 25)
PRONUNCIATION	●	I can use the correct intonation in sentences. (p. 27)
SPEAKING	●	I can add information. (p. 30)
LEARNING OUTCOME	●	I can give a presentation that describes some good ways to make friends, including details and examples. (p. 28)

LISTENING	●	listening for examples
VOCABULARY	●	using the dictionary: antonyms
GRAMMAR	●	adjectives; adverbs + adjectives
PRONUNCIATION	●	sentence stress
SPEAKING	●	giving opinions

Unit QUESTION

What makes a good school?

PREVIEW THE UNIT

A Answer the questions about your school. Then compare with a partner.

1. How many students go to your school? _____

2. How many students are in your class? _____

3. What are two clubs at your school? _____

    _____

4. What are two sports teams at your school? _____

    _____

B Look at the photo. Where are the students? What are they doing?

C Discuss the Unit Question above with your classmates.

🔊 Listen to *The Q Classroom*, Track 21 on CD 1, to hear other answers.

LISTENING | Let's Take a Tour

VOCABULARY

A. Here are some words from the Listening. Read the sentences. Which explanation is correct? Circle *a* or *b*.

1. My university has a big **campus**. It has over 100 buildings.
   a. A campus is all the buildings and areas at a school.
   b. A campus is the students and the teachers at a school.

Tip for Success

The word *school* can refer to any educational institute. The words *college* and *university* often have the same meaning.

2. Matt doesn't have **Internet access** in his room. He goes to a café to check his email.
   a. Matt can go online in his room.
   b. Matt can't go online in his room.

3. Mary has a great math **professor**. His classes are always interesting.
   a. A professor is a university student.
   b. A professor is a university teacher.

4. John gets good grades, so he is in **special** classes. His classes are difficult.
   a. John's classes are different or unusual.
   b. John's classes are normal or regular.

5. James is **active**. He plays soccer and basketball. He also belongs to the Spanish club.
   a. James does a lot of things.
   b. James has a lot of friends.

6. Writing is an important **skill**. Emma writes every day. She wants to be a good writer.
   a. Playing guitar is also a skill.
   b. Watching television is also a skill.

7. David is from France. For David, Korean is a **foreign language**.
   a. French is a foreign language for David.
   b. Spanish is a foreign language for David.

8. A **community** is a group of people. They live or work in the same area.
   a. A bus stop is a kind of community.
   b. A town is a kind of community.

B. Complete the sentences with words from Activity A. (You will not use all the words.)

1. At my school, all of the students study a _____. I'm in a Japanese class.

2. Rob's university has a really small _____. You can walk across it in ten minutes.

3. A class is a kind of _____. The teachers and students work together.

4. I have to talk to my biology _____. I have a question about the test.

5. My brother is very _____. He takes five classes, plays soccer, and is a volunteer.

6. Reading is an important _____. Good students read well.

PREVIEW THE LISTENING

Let's Take a Tour

A. You are going to listen to Sarah Carter, a student, give a tour of Watson University. Look at the map. Then match the names of the places with the definitions.

Watson University

1. library _____   a. Students live here.

2. dormitory _____   b. Students play games here.

3. sports field _____   c. There are a lot of books here.

4. dining commons _____   d. Students eat here.

B. Does your school have the four places in Activity A? What are some other places at your school?

COMPREHENSION CHECK

CD 1
Track 22

A. Read the sentences. Listen to the tour. Write *T* (true) or *F* (false) for each statement. Then correct each false statement to make it true.

_____ 1. There is free Internet access in the dining commons.

_____ 2. About half of the students live on campus.

_____ 3. The school has about 2,000 students.

_____ 4. The professors want students to sit and listen quietly.

_____ 5. The university is in a small town.

_____ 6. Students spend a lot of time in town.

Skill Review	Listening for examples

> In Activity B, you listen for examples. Remember to listen for the expressions *for example* and *like*. Review the Listening Skill box in Unit 2, page 24.

CD 1
Track 22

B. What does Sarah say? Read the questions. Then listen again. Circle the correct answers.

1. What teams does Watson University have?
   a. lacrosse and soccer
   b. football and lacrosse
   c. football and tennis
   d. soccer and tennis

2. Why are small classes important?
   a. Small classes are very quiet.
   b. Small classes are busy.
   c. Professors know the students well.
   d. Professors talk a lot.

3. At Watson University, students are active. What example does Sarah give?
   a. They make special lessons.
   b. They give presentations.
   c. They have discussion groups.
   d. They work alone.

4. Students learn important skills. What example does Sarah give?
   a. study skills
   b. listening skills
   c. speaking skills
   d. writing skills

5. How can students help the community in the town of Watson?
   a. go to dinner
   b. become volunteers
   c. go to a movie
   d. teach foreign languages

Tip for Success

Learning antonyms is a good way to build your vocabulary quickly. When you learn a new adjective, try to find out what its antonym is. Learners' dictionaries often give useful synonyms and antonyms.

Antonyms are words with opposite meanings. For example, *good* and *bad* are antonyms. Most forms of words—nouns, verbs, adjectives, adverbs, and prepositions—can have antonyms.

The dictionary often gives antonyms in the definition of a word. In the example below, notice the antonym of *hard*.

> **hard¹** /hɑrd/ *adjective* (hard·er, hard·est)
> **1** not soft: *These apples are very hard.* ◆ *I couldn't sleep because the bed was too hard.* ➲ **ANTONYM soft**
> **2** difficult to do or understand: *The exam was very hard.* ◆ *hard work* ➲ **ANTONYM easy**
> **3** full of problems: *He's had **a hard life**.* ➲ **ANTONYM easy**
> **4** not kind or gentle: *She is very **hard on** her children.* ➲ **ANTONYM soft**

All dictionary entries are from the *Oxford Basic American Dictionary for learners of English* © Oxford University Press 2011.

A. Write an antonym for each word. Use the words in the box. Use your dictionary to help you.

above	cheap	negative	strength
badly	complicated	easy	succeed

1. hard _____

2. fail _____

3. below _____

4. weakness _____

5. positive _____

6. simple _____

7. expensive _____

8. well _____

We have many discussions.

B. Read each sentence. Circle the correct word.

1. Sun-Hee doesn't like her school. The classrooms are always (clean / dirty).

2. In my history class, we have many discussions and presentations. I like it a lot. It's very (interesting / boring).

3. One (strength / weakness) of my school is the library. It's very small, and it doesn't have a lot of books.

4. The school is in a (safe / dangerous) part of town. Don't go out late at night.

5. My school costs a lot of money. It's very (cheap / **expensive**).

6. In a good school, all of the students (fail / **succeed**).

7. Sarah lives (**on** / off) campus. Her dormitory is near the library.

8. My math class is really (**easy** / hard). I know all of the answers.

C. Choose three adjectives. In your notebook, write a sentence for each adjective and its antonym.

My chemistry class is <u>hard</u>.   Math is <u>easy</u> for me.

 ## WHAT DO YOU THINK?

A. Give your opinion of the following statements. Circle *Yes* or *No*.

What makes a good school?

1. Yes   No   It's important to learn a foreign language in school.

2. Yes   No   It's important to have good friends at school.

3. Yes   No   Every school needs a lot of clubs and teams.

4. Yes   No   A good school has computers for students to use.

5. Yes   No   Every campus needs a library and a sports field.

6. Yes   No   Good schools have small classes.

7. Yes   No   A good school has a large campus.

8. Yes   No   A good school is a community.

9. Yes   No   A good school has new buildings.

10. Yes   No   Good schools are always in big cities.

11. Yes   No   In good schools, students can talk to teachers outside of class.

12. Yes   No   In a good class, students can ask the teacher questions.

 **Critical Thinking**

In Activity B, you **discuss** your answers. This helps you understand the information better.

B. Discuss your answers with a partner. Tell your partner your reasons for your opinions.

A: Is it important to learn a foreign language in school?

B: Yes, it is. You learn about different countries, too.

Adjectives

1. Adjectives describe nouns (people, places, or things).

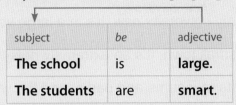

subject	*be*	adjective
The school	is	**large.**
The students	are	**smart.**

- An adjective can come after the verb *be*. It describes the subject.

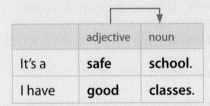

	adjective	noun
It's a	**safe**	**school.**
I have	**good**	**classes.**

- An adjective can come before a noun. It describes the noun.

2. There are no singular or plural adjectives.

   ✓ Correct: They are **interesting classes.**
   ✗ Incorrect: They are interestings classes.

3. Do not use an article (*the*, *a*, or *an*) before an adjective with no noun.

   ✓ Correct: The class is **interesting.**
   ✗ Incorrect: The class is an interesting.

Adverbs + adjectives

1. Adverbs make adjectives stronger.

   It's a **pretty <u>interesting</u>** class.   It's a **very <u>safe</u>** school.
   That school is **really <u>safe</u>**!   This classroom is **extremely <u>noisy</u>**!

   - Use *pretty* in speaking and informal writing. Don't use it in papers for your classes.

2. You can use *pretty*, *really*, *very*, and *extremely* before:

   an adjective alone: That school is **really excellent.**
   an adjective + a noun: It's a **very active class.**

A. Read the paragraph. Find the ten adjective and adverb errors and correct them.

> From: David Baker
> To: Carlos Diaz
> Subject: My school
>
>   *new university*
> Well, I am now at my ~~university new~~. It's in a large very city. It's pretty different from our small town. It's an extremely noisy, but I love it. There are excellents museums and parks, and the weather is perfect. The school doesn't have dormitories. I live in an apartment expensive in the city. The apartment building is beautiful really, but it's pretty old. I have a really great roommate. His name is Joe. My school is great, but my classes are big extremely. Some of my classes have 200 people in them! However, my professors are a very good and my classes are really interesting. We have a science laboratory great. I study biology there. I'm learning a lot. Also, the people here are friendly very, but I miss my old friends.

B. Complete the conversation with adjectives or adverbs + adjectives. Use your own ideas. Then practice with a partner.

the school campus

A: Do you like this school?

B: Yes, I do. I think that it's a _____ _____ school. What do you think?

A: I like it, too. The teachers are _____ and the classes are

_____.

B: What do you think of the library?

A: I think that it's _____ _____ What do you think of the campus?

B: I think that it's _____ _____.

When you speak, you **stress** certain **important words**. This means you say them more loudly.

- Important words—like nouns, adjectives, and adverbs—give the information in the sentences.
- You do not usually stress words like pronouns, prepositions, *a/an/the*, the verb *be*, or the verb *do*.

CD 1
Track 23

> There are **two sports fields**.
> The **museum** is **not interesting**.
> We **go** to **school** in a **really dangerous neighborhood**.
> Do you **have** a **class today**?

CD 1
Track 24

A. Underline the stressed words. Listen and check your answers. Then practice the sentences with a partner.

1. Does the school have a lacrosse team?

2. I have two classes in the morning.

3. We want a safe and clean school.

4. The college is in a dangerous city.

5. The coffee shops have free Internet access.

6. What is a good school?

7. Our sports field is pretty big.

8. My school is really great!

9. The buses to his school are very slow.

10. When does the class begin?

lacrosse team

B. In your notebook, write five sentences about your school. Use adjectives and the adverbs *pretty, really, very,* and *extremely.*

C. Trade papers with a partner. Underline the stressed words. Then practice the sentences.

The <u>campus</u> is <u>extremely</u> <u>large</u>.

CD 1
Track 25

Use the phrases *I think that* . . . and *In my opinion,* . . . to give an opinion.

I think that students need computers.

In my opinion, small classes are important.

You can answer opinions with *I agree* or *I disagree* followed by your opinion.

A: **I think that** our school is great.

B: **I agree.** I think that the classes are interesting.

C: **I disagree.** In my opinion, the classes are too big.

CD 1
Track 26

A. Listen and complete the conversations. Use expressions from the box above. Compare answers with a partner.

1. A: _____ a good school gives a lot of tests.

   Then students study every day.

   B: _____. Class discussions make students study.

2. A: _____ sports are really important. Students

   need healthy bodies.

   B: _____. Exercise is very important.

Tip for Success

When you write *In my opinion*, use a comma. Don't use a comma after *I think that*.

3. A: _____ the food in our dining commons

   isn't very good. I don't like it!

   B: _____. _____ it

   tastes terrible. I usually cook my own food.

4. A: _____ we need a new library. The building

   is really old.

   B: _____. I like our library.

   _____ it's beautiful.

5. **A:** Our school isn't in a good neighborhood.
_____ it's very dangerous. I hear police sirens all the time.

   B: _____. You hear sirens because the police station is on the same street! _____ the school is very safe.

B. Write answers to the questions. Start your answers with _I think that_ or _In my opinion_. Then ask and answer the questions with a partner.

1. What is the perfect number of students in a foreign language class?

   _____

2. In your opinion, what makes a class interesting? Give two ideas.

   _____

3. Do you think it's better to work alone or in a group? Why?

   _____

Unit Assignment | **Plan a perfect school**

 In this assignment, you plan a perfect school and present your plan to your class. This can be a high school, university, or other kind of school. As you prepare, think about the Unit Question, "What makes a good school?" and use the Self-Assessment checklist on page 44.

CONSIDER THE IDEAS

 CD 1 Track 27

Listen to a group present their ideas for a perfect school. Check (✓) the ideas that they give. Then compare answers with a partner.

☐ 1. The perfect school is large.
☐ 2. The classes are very small.
☐ 3. The school has a lot of clubs, like a movie club and a soccer club.
☐ 4. There is a big gym.
☐ 5. Students get free computers.
☐ 6. The school is in a big city.
☐ 7. Apartments in town are cheap and beautiful.
☐ 8. Food on campus is cheap.

PREPARE AND SPEAK

Tip for Success

When you give an opinion, give examples and add information. This makes your opinions stronger and clearer. *I think that a good school needs a sports field, like a soccer field. Students need exercise. It makes them healthy.*

A. GATHER IDEAS **Work in a group of four. Answer these questions. Write your answers in your notebook. Use *I think that* and *In my opinion*, to share your ideas.**

1. Is your perfect school big or small? How many students are in a class?

2. What does the school have? For example, does it have a swimming pool? Does it have computers?

3. Is your school in a big city or a small town? What can students do in the city or town?

4. What is special about your school? How is it different from other schools?

B. ORGANIZE IDEAS **Work with your group. Prepare your presentation.**

1. Each group member chooses one question from Activity A.

2. Write your part of the presentation. Include at least one example or detail for your idea.

3. First speaker: Use these sentences as your introduction.

   Good [morning, afternoon, evening]. Today we are presenting our plan for the perfect school.

4. Last speaker: Use these sentences as your conclusion.

   That's the end of our presentation. Thank you for listening. Do you have any questions?

C. SPEAK **Present your ideas to your class. Look at the Self-Assessment checklist below before you begin.**

CHECK AND REFLECT

A. CHECK **Think about the Unit Assignment and complete the Self-Assessment checklist.**

		SELF-ASSESSMENT
Yes	**No**	
☐	☐	I gave my opinion clearly.
☐	☐	I used vocabulary from this unit.
☐	☐	I used adjectives and adverbs + adjectives correctly.
☐	☐	I stressed words in sentences correctly.

B. **REFLECT** Discuss these questions with a partner.

1. What is something new you learned in this unit?

2. Think about the Unit Question, "What makes a good school?" What is your opinion now? Is it the same as or different from your opinion at the start of the unit? Explain.

Track Your Success

Circle the words you learned in this unit.

Nouns
campus
community 🔑 AWL
foreign language
Internet access
professor
skill 🔑
strength 🔑
weakness 🔑

Verbs
fail 🔑
succeed 🔑

Adjectives
active 🔑
boring 🔑
cheap 🔑
clean 🔑
complicated 🔑
dangerous 🔑
dirty 🔑
expensive 🔑
hard 🔑
interesting 🔑
negative 🔑 AWL
positive 🔑 AWL
safe 🔑

simple 🔑
special 🔑

Adverbs
badly 🔑
extremely 🔑
pretty 🔑
really 🔑
very 🔑
well 🔑

Prepositions
above 🔑
below 🔑
off 🔑
on 🔑

🔑 Oxford 2000 keywords
AWL Academic Word List

Check (✓) the skills you learned. If you need more work on a skill, refer to the page(s) in parentheses.

LISTENING	○	I can listen for examples. (p. 36)
VOCABULARY	○	I can use the dictionary to understand antonyms. (p. 37)
GRAMMAR	○	I can use adjectives and adverbs + adjectives. (p. 39)
PRONUNCIATION	○	I can use correct sentence stress. (p. 41)
SPEAKING	○	I can give my opinion. (p. 42)
LEARNING OUTCOME	●	I can share my opinions to plan a perfect school and present the plan to the class. (p. 43)

UNIT 4

Food

LISTENING ●	listening for reasons
VOCABULARY ●	prefixes and suffixes
GRAMMAR ●	verbs + gerunds or infinitives
PRONUNCIATION ●	stressed syllables
SPEAKING ●	giving opinions

LEARNING OUTCOME ●

Design a survey about food and interview a classmate about his or her food choices.

Unit QUESTION

How do you choose your food?

PREVIEW THE UNIT

(A) Cross out the adjectives that *don't* describe food. Then compare with a partner.

active	spicy	dangerous
delicious	close	healthy
fresh	important	salty
sour	difficult	sweet

(B) Look at the photo. Where are the people? What words for food do you see?

(C) Discuss the Unit Question above with your classmates.

(») Listen to *The Q Classroom*, Track 28 on CD 1, to hear other answers.

LISTENING

LISTENING | Lifestyles and Food Choices

VOCABULARY

A. Here are some words from the Listening. Read the definitions. Then complete the sentences below.

> **avoid** (*verb*) to try not to do something
> **artificial** (*adjective*) not natural or real; made by people
> **convenient** (*adjective*) easy to get or to use
> **flavor** (*noun*) the taste of food, like salty or sweet
> **nutritious** (*adjective*) good for you
> **organic** (*adjective*) natural; organic food has only natural ingredients
> **social** (*adjective*) a social person likes other people
> **vegetarian** (*noun*) a person—he or she does not eat meat

ingredients

1. Some foods have _____ ingredients in them. They are not 100% natural.

2. Fruits and vegetables are very _____. For example, oranges have a lot of Vitamin C.

3. Rob is a very _____ person. He spends a lot of time with his friends.

4. Amanda and Matt _____ food with a lot of fat. For example, they don't eat French fries or cheeseburgers.

5. Lemons are sour, but oranges have a sweet _____.

6. Sam doesn't eat chicken or beef. He's a _____.

7. John buys his food at a health-food store. He eats only _____ food.

8. Emma is very busy. She eats a lot of fast food. She knows it's bad for her, but it is very _____.

B. Answer the questions. Then compare with a partner.

1. What is an example of a convenient food? _____

2. What is an example of a food with a strong flavor? _____

3. Are you a vegetarian or do you eat meat? _____

4. How often do you eat organic food? _____

5. Do you avoid food with artificial ingredients? _____

   Why or why not? _____

6. Name three foods that are very nutritious. _____

   _____

PREVIEW THE LISTENING

Lifestyles and Food Choices

You are going to listen to a reporter interview four people in a supermarket. She asks, "How do you choose your food?" She learns about the way the people live.

What questions do you think about when you choose your food? Check (✓) the questions.

1. ☐ Is it good for me?

2. ☐ Does it have a lot of sugar in it?

3. ☐ Does it have a lot of fat in it?

4. ☐ Is it organic?

5. ☐ Does it taste good?

6. ☐ How much does it cost?

7. ☐ Is it convenient?

8. ☐ Does it have meat in it?

COMPREHENSION CHECK

CD 1 Track 29 **A.** Listen to the four conversations. Match each person with the correct information.

1. Carlos ___   a. likes cooking.

2. Mika ___   b. listens to his doctor's advice.

3. Matt ___   c. is an athlete.

4. Sarah ___   d. is a busy student.

CD 1 Track 29 **B.** Look at the chart. Then listen again. Check (✓) the correct information about each person.

1. Carlos	2. Mika	3. Matt	4. Sarah	
✓	☐	☐	☐	a. is a vegetarian.
☐	☐	☐	☐	b. eats only organic food.
☐	☐	☐	☐	c. likes to taste new flavors.
☐	☐	☐	☐	d. thinks meat is bad for you.
☐	☐	☐	☐	e. doesn't have a kitchen.
☐	☐	☐	☐	f. is a very social person.
☐	☐	☐	☐	g. avoids food with a lot of fat and salt.
☐	☐	☐	☐	h. eats fast food because it's convenient.
☐	☐	☐	☐	i. eats nutritious food, like fish.
☐	☐	☐	☐	j. is 71 years old.

I'm very careful about food.

A **prefix** comes at the beginning of a word. It changes the meaning of the word. A **suffix** comes at the end of a word. It often changes the part of speech. Learners' dictionaries usually give definitions for prefixes and suffixes. Other dictionaries often list them at the back.

The prefixes *non-* and *un-* mean "not." The suffix *-free* means "without," and it changes a noun (*sugar*) into an adjective (*sugar-free*). Look at their definitions.

Prefix	Suffix
non- not: *a **non**smoker (= a person who does not smoke) • **non**alcoholic drinks (= drinks containing no alcohol) • a **non**stop flight*	**-free** (in adjectives) not containing the bad thing mentioned: *sugar-**free** cola • fat-**free** yogurt • a smoke-**free** environment • a tax-**free** savings account*

Prefix	
un- not; the opposite of: *un**happy** • un**true** (= not true) • un**lock** • un**dress** (= to take clothes off)*	

All dictionary entries are from the *Oxford Basic American Dictionary for learners of English* © Oxford University Press 2011.

A. Read the sentences. Complete each sentence with a word in the box.

nondairy	salt-free	unhealthy	unfriendly
nonfat	sugar-free	unsafe	unusual

☐ 1. I worry about foods with a lot of fat. I drink only

_____ milk.

☐ 2. I eat a lot of junk food, like chips, cookies, and cake. I never exercise.

I'm often sick. I'm very _____.

☐ 3. She doesn't talk to anyone. She's very _____.

☐ 4. I'm allergic to food with milk, cheese, or butter. I eat only

_____ food.

I'm allergic to food with milk.

☐ 5. I don't eat food with a lot of salt in it. Salt is bad for my health. I try to eat _____ food.

☐ 6. I only eat organic food. I think food with artificial ingredients is _____.

☐ 7. I avoid food and drinks with sugar. I try to have only _____ food and drinks.

☐ 8. I like to try _____ foods. I don't like to eat the same kind of food every day.

INGREDIENTS: Flour (bleache grade potassium bromate, ma (Interesterfied soybean oil, m diglycerides, lecithin, sodium (preservative), artificial flavor, hydrogenated palm oil, caram propylene glycol, tricalcium pl sodium bicarbonate, salt, pro

artificial ingredients

B. Check (✓) the items in Activity A that are true for you. Then compare your answers with a partner.

C. Find three words with *non-*, *un-*, or *-free* in your dictionary. In your notebook, write three true sentences about your life with those words.

| Pronunciation | Stressed syllables | |

CD 1 Track 30

In words with two or more syllables, you usually **stress one syllable**. You say the syllable with more energy. In these words, the bold syllables are stressed.

or • **gan** • ic   veg • e • **tar** • i • an   un • **friend** • ly

CD 1 Track 31

A. Listen to the words. Circle the stressed syllables. Then practice with a partner.

1. de • li • cious
2. al • ler • gic
3. un • health • y
4. ed • u • ca • tion
5. con • ven • ient

6. su • gar • free
7. gar • den
8. din • ner
9. non • dai • ry
10. com • mu • ni • ty

B. Listen to the sentences. Circle the stressed syllables in words with two
or more syllables.

 for Success

We usually don't
stress words
like pronouns,
prepositions, and
articles. See the
Pronunciation box
on page 41 for
more information.

1. In my opinion, artificial ingredients are unsafe.

2. He doesn't eat chicken or beef.

3. He wants to lose weight, so he's on a diet.

4. This soup has an unusual flavor.

5. Are these cookies sugar-free?

6. She grows organic tomatoes in her garden.

 CD 1
Track 33

C. Listen again. Underline the stressed words in the sentences.

| Listening Skill | Listening for reasons | |

 CD 1
Track 34

Speakers use reasons to explain their actions. In conversations, speakers often
use **why** to ask for reasons. They use **because** to give reasons.

A: **Why** do you eat sugar-free food?   A: **Why** don't you eat fast food?

B: **Because** sugar is bad for your teeth.   B: **Because** it has artificial
ingredients in it.

Listen for these two key words—*why* and *because*—to understand reasons.

 CD 1
Track 35

A. Read the sentences. Then listen to the conversations. Circle the
answer to each question.

1. Why does John buy only organic apples?
   a. Because they are cheap.
   b. Because they're good for him.
   c. Because he likes the flavor.

2. Why does Amanda avoid fattening foods?
   a. Because she doesn't like them.
   b. Because she wants to lose weight.
   c. Because they're bad for her health.

fattening foods

3. Why does James want to go out for dinner?

   a. Because his friend is a terrible cook.

   b. Because he is a terrible cook.

   c. Because he doesn't have any food at home.

4. Kay's Kitchen is Anna's favorite restaurant. Why?

   a. Because it's near her house.

   b. Because their food is delicious.

   c. Because their food is cheap.

B. **Are you similar to John, Amanda, James, or Anna? Choose one person. Tell your classmates.**

I think I'm similar to John. We both like organic food.

 WHAT DO YOU THINK?

A. Answer these questions.

FOOD SURVEY

1. Do you eat meat? Why or why not?

2. Do you eat fast food? Why or why not?

3. Do you eat organic food? Why or why not?

4. Do you eat food with artificial ingredients? Why or why not?

5. What kind of food do you usually eat? Why do you choose it?

6. What's your favorite food? Why?

7. What kinds of food do you avoid? Why?

8. What do you usually eat for breakfast?

 for Success

You can use *Why don't you . . . ?* or *Why doesn't he/ she . . . ?* to ask why someone <u>doesn't</u> do something.

B. Discuss your answers with a partner.

A: Do you eat meat?

B: Yes, I do.

A: Why?

B: Because it's delicious and I like the flavor.

SPEAKING

Verbs + gerunds or infinitives

1. Gerunds and infinitives are usually words for activities.
   - A gerund is a **base verb** + **-ing**: *eating, cooking, baking*
   - An infinitive is **to** + **a base verb**: *to eat, to cook, to bake*

2. **Verbs + gerunds** You can use gerunds after these verbs.

subject	verb	gerund
We	**enjoy**	**cooking.**
I	**avoid**	**buying** fast food.

3. **Verbs + infinitives** You can use infinitives after these verbs.

subject	verb	infinitive
He	**tries**	**to eat** only organic food.
We	**need**	**to make** dinner.
They	**want**	**to eat** only healthy food.

4. **Verbs + gerunds or infinitives** You can use gerunds or infinitives after these verbs.

subject	verb	gerund or infinitive
He	likes	**to eat** at home. **eating** at home.
We	hate	**to shop** at Bob's Market. **shopping** at Bob's Market.
They	love	**to go** out to dinner. **going out** to dinner.
I	can't stand	**to cook** **cooking.**

A. Listen to the sentences. What do you hear? Circle the gerund
or infinitive.

1. (to cook)/ cooking   6. to avoid / avoiding

2. to eat / eating   7. to cook / cooking

3. to shop / shopping   8. to eat / eating

4. to buy / buying   9. to eat / eating

5. to eat / eating   10. to go / going

B. Complete the conversation with the correct infinitive or gerund forms.
In some sentences, both a gerund and an infinitive are correct.

Mary and Sun-Hee

Mary: Sun-Hee, I have to make dinner for my husband's parents on Friday

night. I'm so nervous. Can you help me?

Sun-Hee: Sure, I love _____ (cook). What kinds of food do
                                1

they like _____ (eat)?
                2

Mary: Well, my mother-in-law enjoys _____ (try) new
                                              3

things, but my father-in-law avoids _____ (eat) a lot of
                                          4

different things. For example, he's allergic to dairy foods, and he tries

_____ (avoid) foods with a lot of salt.
      5

Sun-Hee: What do they like?

Mary: Um, they like chicken and fish. And they like vegetables.

Sun-Hee: All right. I have a great recipe for roast chicken and vegetables.

It's spicy, but it's not very salty.

Mary: That sounds perfect! Thanks so much. I try _____
                                                            6

(cook), but I'm not very good in the kitchen.

Sun-Hee: No problem. What time do you want _____ (start)?
                                                        7

Mary: How about 3:00?

Sun-Hee: Great! I'll see you then!

C. Complete the sentences with information about food. Use an infinitive or gerund in each sentence. Share your ideas with a partner.

Possible verbs						
avoid	bake	buy	cook	drink	eat	feel
find	go	grow	have	listen	make	tell

1. I want _____

2. I need _____

3. I avoid _____

4. I try _____

5. I like _____

6. I love _____

7. I hate _____

8. I enjoy _____

Unit Assignment   Design a survey and interview a classmate

 In this assignment, you make a survey and interview a classmate about his or her food choices. As you prepare, think about the Unit Question, "How do you choose your food?" and use the Self-Assessment checklist on page 58.

CONSIDER THE IDEAS

CD 1
Track 37

Listen to the interview. Match the questions to the student's answers.

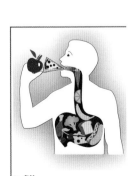

It fills me up.

1. What's your favorite food? ____

2. Do you think organic food is good for you? ____

3. Why do you avoid strawberries? ____

4. What do you usually eat for breakfast? ____

5. Why do you choose nonfat yogurt? ____

a. Because I'm allergic to them.

b. Nonfat yogurt.

c. I don't know.

d. Because it fills me up and gives me energy.

e. Pizza.

PREPARE AND SPEAK

A. GATHER IDEAS Work with a partner. Write ten interview questions in your notebook.

- Write questions about food likes, dislikes, choices, and opinions.
- Include questions with gerunds and infinitives.

B. ORGANIZE IDEAS Work with your partner and prepare your survey.

1. Look at your ten questions from Activity A. Circle your four best questions. Include at least one opinion question.

2. Write your questions in your notebook. Leave room for answers and follow-up questions.

Skill Review   Giving opinions

 for Success

When you want more information, you can ask **a follow-up question**. For example:

Why is it your favorite? Why not?

When you are answering an interviewer's questions, remember to use the phrases *In my opinion*, and *I think that* to give your opinion. Review the Speaking Skill box in Unit 3, page 42.

C. SPEAK Follow these steps. Look at the Self-Assessment checklist below before you begin.

1. Each partner works individually. Use the questions to interview another student in your class. Write down his or her answers.

Tip Critical Thinking

Activity C asks you to tell the class about your answers. You have to **summarize** the information. This shows you understand the ideas.

2. Work with your partner. Compare your answers. How are the answers the same or different? Share your ideas with the class.

CHECK AND REFLECT

A. CHECK Think about the Unit Assignment and complete the Self-Assessment checklist.

SELF-ASSESSMENT		
Yes	No	
☐	☐	Our interview questions were clear.
☐	☐	I used vocabulary from this unit.
☐	☐	I used gerunds and infinitives correctly.
☐	☐	I gave reasons for my opinions when answering questions.

B. **REFLECT** Discuss these questions with a partner.

1. What is something new you learned in this unit?

2. Think about the Unit Question, "How do you choose your food?" What are the main reasons for people's food choices?

Track Your Success

Circle the words you learned in this unit.

Nouns	nonstop	**Verbs**
fast food	nutritious	avoid 🔑
flavor 🔑	organic	bake 🔑
ingredients	salt-free	choose 🔑
vegetarian	social 🔑	enjoy 🔑
Adjectives	sugar-free	grow 🔑
allergic (to)	unfriendly 🔑	need 🔑
artificial 🔑	unhealthy	(can't) stand 🔑
convenient 🔑	unsafe	try 🔑
nondairy	unusual 🔑	want 🔑
nonfat		**Conjunction**
		because 🔑

🔑 Oxford 2000 keywords
AWL Academic Word List

Check (✓) the skills you learned. If you need more work on a skill, refer to the page(s) in parentheses.

LISTENING ⚪	I can listen for reasons. (p. 53)
VOCABULARY ⚪	I can use prefixes and suffixes. (p. 51)
GRAMMAR ⚪	I can use gerunds and infinitives correctly. (p. 55)
PRONUNCIATION ⚪	I can recognize stressed syllables. (p. 52)
SPEAKING ⚪	I can give an opinion. (p. 58)
LEARNING OUTCOME ⚪	I can design a survey about food and interview a classmate about his or her food choices. (p. 57)

UNIT 5

Fun

LISTENING ● listening for reasons
VOCABULARY ● collocations with *do*, *play*, and *go*
GRAMMAR ● subject and object pronouns
PRONUNCIATION ● reduced pronouns
SPEAKING ● agreeing and disagreeing

LEARNING OUTCOME

Participate in a group discussion about fun places in your area.

Unit QUESTION

What makes something fun?

PREVIEW THE UNIT

A Complete the chart. Then compare with a partner.

What is . . . ?	
a fun activity	
a boring activity	
an exciting activity	
a dangerous activity	
an interesting activity	

B Look at the photo. What are the people doing? Do you think it looks fun?

C Discuss the Unit Question above with your classmates.

Listen to *The Q Classroom*, Track 38 on CD 1, to hear other answers.

61

LISTENING | ## Why Do You Come to the Park?

VOCABULARY

Here are some words from Listening 1. Read the sentences. Then complete each sentence on page 63 with one of the bold words.

Tom likes **modern** art.

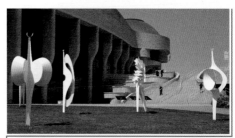
Toshi loves to look at **sculptures**.

Do you want to go to a **concert**?

In the summer, we sometimes eat **outdoors**.

There is a great hiking **path** in the woods near my house.

Sun-Hee likes to be in **nature**. She loves trees and flowers.

James doesn't like **crowded** streets. There are too many people!

Kate likes to read on the weekend. It's very **relaxing**.

1. I like to listen to classical music in the evening. It's _____.

2. I don't like _____ cars. I like older cars.

3 There are a lot of people here! It's really _____.

4. Let's walk on my favorite _____ in the park. It goes around the lake.

5. I love to spend time in _____. I like to look at the trees, the grass, and the animals.

6. This _____ is really great! I love to hear live music.

7. I like to play basketball _____. I don't like to play in a gym.

8. I like to make _____ in my art class.

PREVIEW THE LISTENING

Why Do You Come to the Park?

You are going to listen to a travel reporter talk about Ibirapuera Park (pronounced *ee-BIH-ra-poo-AIR-ah*), a large park in the city of São Paulo, Brazil.

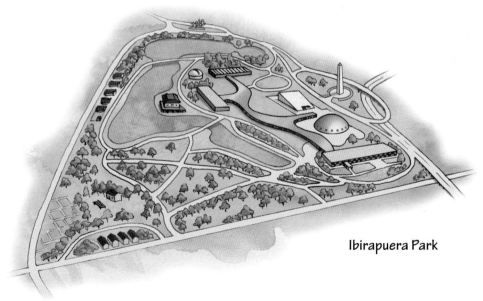

Ibirapuera Park

Look at the list of places. Check (✓) things you think are in Ibirapuera Park.

☐ a beach   ☐ a lake   ☐ paths   ☐ a shopping mall

☐ concerts   ☐ a library   ☐ roads   ☐ sports fields

☐ gardens   ☐ museums   ☐ sculptures   ☐ a swimming pool

Remember: In conversations, speakers often use **why** to ask for reasons. They use **because** to give reasons. Review the Listening Skill box in Unit 4, page 53.

COMPREHENSION CHECK

 CD 1
Track 39

A. Read the sentences. Then listen to the report. Why do Isabel and Carlos come to the park? Check (✓) their reasons.

1. Isabel
   a. ☐ She learns about art.
   b. ☐ She likes to go hiking.
   c. ☐ She loves music.
   d. ☐ She can play sports.

2. Carlos
   a. ☐ It's crowded.
   b. ☐ He likes the museum.
   c. ☐ He wants to do nothing.
   d. ☐ He likes to be active.

 CD 1
Track 39

B. Read the questions. Then listen again. Circle the correct answer.

a sculpture in the park

1. What does Isabel like to look at in the park?
   a. the trees
   b. the gardens
   c. the important buildings
   d. the sculptures

2. Why does Isabel like the concerts?
   a. They're outdoors and they're cheap.
   b. They're outdoors and they're free.
   c. They're in the Museum of Modern Art.
   d. She hears new music.

3. What does Carlos <u>not</u> do in the park?
   a. He doesn't go hiking on the paths.
   b. He doesn't go swimming in the lake.
   c. He doesn't ride his bike with friends.
   d. He doesn't spend time in nature.

4. What does Carlos like to look at?
   a. the trees and gardens
   b. the important buildings
   c. the city around the park
   d. the sculptures and art

Words for activities often follow the verbs *do*, *play*, or *go*.

They **do gymnastics** on Saturdays.
She **plays basketball** at her school.
He **goes skiing** in the mountains.

Do	Play	Go*
do aerobics	play baseball	go hiking
do gymnastics	play chess	go jogging
do judo	play the guitar	go shopping
do nothing	play an instrument	go skiing
do yoga	play video games	go swimming

*You usually use the verb *go* with a gerund (verb + -*ing*).

A. Complete the conversations with *play*, *do*, or *go*.

Tip for Success

The word *let's* introduces suggestions.

1. **Sam:** Emma, I'm bored. Let's do something.

    Emma: Sure. Let's _____ shopping.

    Sam: I don't like shopping. Let's _____ video games.

    Emma: No, I'm not good at video games. Uh, do you want to

    _____ hiking?

    Sam: OK. That's a great idea!

shopping

2. **John:** Mike, I want to lose weight. What do you do for exercise?

   Mike: I _____ judo. I have a class twice a week.

   John: Do you still _____ gymnastics?

   Mike: No, it was too difficult.

judo

3. **Hassan:** Toshi, do you want to _____ swimming with me?

   Toshi: No, thanks. I have a music lesson.

   Hassan: Oh, do you _____ an instrument?

   Toshi: Yes, I _____ the guitar. Hey, do you want to

   _____ skiing this weekend?

   Hassan: Sure, that sounds like fun!

skiing

 Critical Thinking

In Activity B,
you **practice** the
collocations. This
helps you remember
vocabulary better.

B. Answer the questions with information about yourself. Include the verbs *play*, *do*, or *go* in every sentence. Then ask and answer the questions with a partner.

1. **A:** What do you like to do on weekends?

    B: I like to _____.

2. **A:** What do you like to do at night?

    B: I like to _____.

3. **A:** What else do you like to do for fun?

    B: I like to _____.

4. **A:** What do you hate to do?

    B: I really hate to _____.

 WHAT DO YOU THINK?

A. Give your opinion about fun. Circle *Yes* or *No* for each sentence.

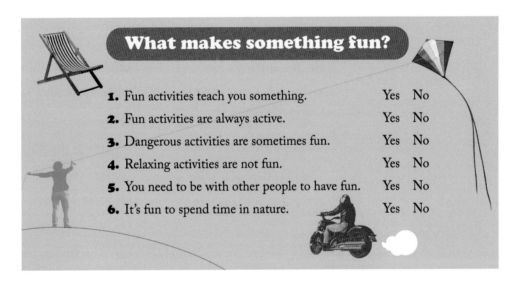

What makes something fun?

1. Fun activities teach you something.   Yes   No
2. Fun activities are always active.   Yes   No
3. Dangerous activities are sometimes fun.   Yes   No
4. Relaxing activities are not fun.   Yes   No
5. You need to be with other people to have fun. Yes   No
6. It's fun to spend time in nature.   Yes   No

B. Compare your ideas with a partner.

1. Look at Activity A. How many times do you and your partner have the same answer?

2. What two activities do you and your partner both enjoy?

    We both like to . . . and . . .

3. Does *fun* mean the same thing to you and your partner?

Grammar | **Subject and object pronouns**

1. Subjects and objects can be nouns.
   - Subjects come before verbs in statements.
   - Objects come after verbs or prepositions, like *at*, *in*, and *on*.

subject	verb	object	preposition + object
Kate	likes	the **book**.	
My **brother**	runs	—	in the **park**.

2. Pronouns replace nouns.
   - You use some pronouns for subjects.
   - You use other pronouns for objects.

	subject pronoun	object pronoun
singular	**I** have a great soccer coach.	She helps **me**.
	You are good at swimming.	I want to go with **you**.
	He goes hiking a lot.	I sometimes see **him** in the park.
	She is good at tennis.	I like playing with **her**.
	I like the park. **It's** really big.	My friends like **it** too.
plural	**We** see movies on Sundays.	Our friends meet **us** at the theater.
	You play baseball a lot.	I sometimes see **you** at the field.
	They are great singers.	I like to listen to **them**.

3. You usually use pronouns *he/him*, *she/her*, *it/it*, *we/us*, and *they/them* after you know the noun.

Mary knows Tom well. **She** studies with **him** every Friday.

(Mary = **she**; Tom = **him**)

A. Circle the correct pronoun.

1. (He / Him) goes hiking on Saturdays.

2. Let's see a movie with (they / them) tomorrow.

3. (We / Us) like to spend time in the park.

4. Sarah's friends make (she / her) laugh.

5. I like this sculpture. (He / It) is beautiful.

6. John and (I / me) love to play chess.

7. James plays baseball with Sam and (I / me).

8. Fun activities sometimes teach (we / us) something.

B. Complete each sentence with a pronoun for the underlined word.

1. That TV <u>show</u> is really exciting. I watch _____ every week.

2. Isabel's <u>sister</u> loves to go hiking. _____ goes every weekend.

3. The free <u>concerts</u> are wonderful. I really love _____.

4. I see my <u>grandmother</u> on Wednesdays. I have lunch with _____.

5. My <u>classes</u> are very interesting, but _____ are difficult.

6. <u>Sun-Hee and Mary</u> go jogging in the park. Then _____ have lunch.

7. <u>We</u> play basketball in the gym. Sometimes, our friends join _____.

8. I want to play tennis with <u>you</u>. _____ are an excellent player.

C. Look back at Activities A and B. Write an *S* over all the subject pronouns. Write an *O* over all the object pronouns.

D. Complete the conversation with the correct subject and object pronouns.

Sarah: Maria, how do _____ like your judo class?
1

Maria: I love _____! My teacher is great. She's from Japan and
2

_____ really knows judo. What's new with you?
3

Sarah: I'm taking an art class.

Maria: Oh, do _____ paint?
4

Sarah: No, but _____ draw. I also make sculptures. The class
5

is really fun. I like the other students. _____ are very talented.
6

Maria: That's great. Hey, my friends and I are going to the beach

this weekend. Do _____ want to come with
7

_____ ?
8

Sarah: Sure, that sounds fun and relaxing.

Pronunciation   **Reduced pronouns**   web

CD 1
Track 40

You usually say pronouns quickly, with no stress. When you say *he, him, her,*
and *them,* you don't usually pronounce the beginning sounds. You "**reduce**"
the words.

   I think **he**'s at the park.   I don't see **him**.
   Is that **her** bike?   Let's call **them**.

You <u>do</u> pronounce the "h" of *he* when it's the first word in a sentence.

   He's at the park.

A. Complete the conversations with *he*, *him*, *her*, and *them*. Then listen and check your answers. Practice the conversations with a partner. Say the reduced forms.

1. **A:** John is a fun guy. How do you know _____? Does

    _____ play soccer with you?

    B: No. I know _____ from school. How do you know

    _____?

    A: _____ spends time at the park near my house.

    Sometimes _____ plays basketball there with my

    friends and me.

2. **A:** Anna's sister Emma is here this weekend. Do you know

    _____?

    B: Yes, I do. I really like _____.

    A: Me too. Do you think Anna and Emma want to see a movie

    with us tonight?

    B: Maybe. Let's call _____.

B. Write four sentences with *he*, *him*, *her*, and *them*. Then take turns reading your sentences with a partner.

1. _____

2. _____

3. _____

4. _____

Speaking Skill Agreeing and disagreeing

CD 1
Track 42

Use these expressions to **agree** with another person's opinion.

Agreeing with a positive opinion	Agreeing with a negative opinion
A: I like swimming. B: **I do too. / Me too.***	A: I don't like swimming. B: **I don't either. / Me neither.***

* *Me too* and *Me neither* sound more informal.

Use these expressions to **disagree** with another person's opinion. These expressions sound more friendly or polite.

Disagreeing politely
A: I think that the sculpture is pretty. B: **Oh, I don't know.**
A: I love that park. How about you? B: **I'm not sure.**

I do too.

I'm not sure.

CD 1
Track 43

A. Listen to the short conversations. Check (✓) *Agree* or *Disagree* for each conversation. Then listen again and write the expression that you hear.

	Agree	Disagree	Expression
1.	☐	☐	
2.	☐	☐	
3.	☐	☐	
4.	☐	☐	
5.	☐	☐	
6.	☐	☐	

B. Write six sentences about things that you like or don't like. Then read them to a partner. Your partner will agree or disagree.

1. I really like _____.

2. I don't like _____.

3. I think _____.

4. I think _____.

5. I enjoy _____.

4. I hate _____.

A: I really like to stay home and do nothing.
B: I do too.

| **Unit Assignment** | **Participate in a group discussion about fun places in your area** |

Q In this assignment, you have a group discussion about the "Top Five" fun places in your area. As you prepare, think about the unit question, "What makes something fun?" and use the Self-Assessment checklist on page 74.

CONSIDER THE IDEAS

CD 1
Track 44 **A.** Listen to a group discuss the fun places in their area. What places do they talk about? Check (✓) the six places. Then compare with a partner.

☐ 1. the city park ☐ 6. the Modern Art Museum

☐ 2. the swimming pool ☐ 7. the shopping mall

☐ 3. the movie theater ☐ 8. the beach

☐ 4. the gym ☐ 9. downtown

☐ 5. the concert hall ☐ 10. a sculpture garden

B. Do you agree with the answers in Activity A? Are they fun places? Which places do you think are fun? Discuss your answers with a partner.

PREPARE AND SPEAK

A. **GATHER IDEAS** What are your five favorite places in your area? Complete the chart with your ideas. Give reasons for each place.

	Name of fun place	Why is it a fun place?
1.		
2.		
3.		
4.		
5.		

Tip for Success

You can share ideas and give suggestions with expressions *How about . . . ?* and *What about . . . ?*

B. **ORGANIZE IDEAS** Choose three ideas from Activity A. Practice different ways to share your ideas. You can use these phrases.

I think that the park is a really fun place because there's a lake and hiking paths.

How about the park? It has a lake and hiking paths.

C. **SPEAK** Work in a group. Discuss your ideas. Look at the Self-Assessment checklist below before you begin.

- Share your three places and your reasons.
- Listen carefully to others' ideas. Agree and disagree with them.
- As a group, choose the best five places.

CHECK AND REFLECT

A. **CHECK** Think about the Unit Assignment and complete the Self-Assessment checklist.

		SELF-ASSESSMENT
Yes	No	
☐	☐	My information was clear.
☐	☐	I used vocabulary from this unit.
☐	☐	I used subject and object pronouns correctly.
☐	☐	I used expressions for agreeing and disagreeing.
☐	☐	I used reduced words correctly.

B. REFLECT Discuss these questions with a partner.

1. What is something new you learned in this unit?

2. Think about the Unit Question, "What makes something fun?" Do you have a different opinion now? If yes, how is your opinion different?

Track Your Success

Circle the words you learned in this unit.

Nouns	**Collocations**	**Pronouns**
concert 🔑	do aerobics	I - me 🔑
nature 🔑	do gymnastics	he - him 🔑
path 🔑	do judo	it - it 🔑
sculpture	do nothing	she - her 🔑
	do yoga	they - them 🔑
Adjectives	go jogging	we - us 🔑
crowded	go skiing	you - you 🔑
modern 🔑	go swimming	
relaxing AWL	play an instrument	
	play baseball	
Adverb		
outdoors		

🔑 Oxford 2000 keywords
AWL Academic Word List

Check (✓) the skills you learned. If you need more work on a skill, refer to the page(s) in parentheses.

LISTENING ○	I can listen for reasons. (p. 64)
VOCABULARY ○	I can understand collocations with *do, play,* and *go.* (p. 65)
GRAMMAR ○	I can use subject and object pronouns correctly. (p. 68)
PRONUNCIATION ○	I can reduce the pronouns *he, him, her,* and *them.* (p. 70)
SPEAKING ○	I can agree and disagree. (p. 72)
LEARNING OUTCOME ○	I can participate in a group discussion about fun places in my area. (p. 73)

LEARNING OUTCOME

Design your perfect home and present your design to the class.

Unit QUESTION

What makes a good home?

PREVIEW THE UNIT

(A) Discuss these questions with a partner.

1. Which words are <u>not</u> places to live? Cross them out. Then compare.

apartment	garage	house	office	restaurant
dormitory	hotel	mansion	park	studio

2. What kind of place do you live in? Use two adjectives to describe it.

I live in a big house. It's very modern.

(B) Look at the photo. What kinds of buildings do you see? Which buildings look like good places to live in?

(C) Discuss the Unit Question above with your classmates.

)) Listen to *The Q Classroom*, Track 2 on CD 2, to hear other answers.

LISTENING

LISTENING 1 | How Do You Like Your Home?

VOCABULARY

Here are some words from Listening 1. Read the sentences. Which explanation is correct? Circle *a* or *b*.

Tip) for Success

House and *home* can have different meanings. Both words mean a building where someone lives. But a *home* can also be a place where someone feels comfortable or a place where someone originally comes from.

1. Rob plays loud music in his apartment. His apartment is **noisy**.
   a. Rob's apartment is quiet.
   b. Rob's apartment isn't quiet.

2. Anna likes her **private** room, but she sometimes gets lonely.
   a. Anna doesn't share her room with someone.
   b. Anna shares her room with someone.

3. Matt's apartment is in a great **location**. It's on a quiet street near his school.
   a. His apartment is cheap and very large.
   b. His apartment is in a convenient place.

4. Sarah has a **comfortable** chair. She likes to sit in it.
   a. The chair is very soft.
   b. The chair is very hard.

5. David's **rent** is really expensive, so he wants to get a roommate.
   a. David's apartment is free.
   b. David pays a lot of money for his apartment.

6. Mika and Sun-Hee are **roommates**. They both live in Room 215.
   a. Mika and Sun-Hee live together.
   b. Mika and Sun-Hee have a class together.

7. Isabel lives with her **extended family**, including her parents, her grandmother and grandfather, and two cousins.
   a. Isabel lives with many family members.
   b. Isabel lives with some friends from school.

8. Our city doesn't have **public transportation**. People usually walk or drive.
   a. The city has no streets or sidewalks.
   b. The city has no buses or trains.

PREVIEW LISTENING 1

How Do You Like Your Home?

You are going to listen to Amanda talk to her friends. She wants to move closer to school, and she wants some advice.

Write two good things about your home and two bad things about your home.

I like my roommates.

My apartment is noisy.

Good: _____

_____

Bad: _____

_____

COMPREHENSION CHECK

CD 2
Track 3

A. Listen to the three conversations. Write the correct name below each picture. In general, does the person like his or her home? Check (✓) *Likes* or *Dislikes*.

Carlos	John	Mary

1. _____ 2. _____ 3. _____

☐ Likes ☐ Dislikes   ☐ Likes ☐ Dislikes   ☐ Likes ☐ Dislikes

B. Look at these statements. Which are good points and which are bad points? Write each statement in the correct part of the chart.

The rent is expensive.	It's far from school.
I don't pay any rent.	It's near public transportation.
It's noisy.	I like the people I live with.
It's comfortable.	It's not private.
It's near school and classes.	It's very private.

	1. John	2. Mary	3. Carlos
Good Points:			
1.	☐	☐	☐
2.	☐	☐	☐
3.	☐	☐	☐
4.	☐	☐	☐
5.	☐	☐	☐
6.	☐	☐	☐
Bad Points:			
7.	☐	☐	☐
8.	☐	☐	☐
9.	☐	☐	☐
10.	☐	☐	☐

CD 2
Track 3

Listen again. Check (✓) the correct name for each point in the chart. You will check some items more than once.

C. Which home do you like? John's, Mary's, or Carlos's? Why?

I like _____'s home because . . .

Q WHAT DO YOU THINK?

Tip **Critical Thinking**

The *What Do You Think?* activity asks you to **rank** items. Ranking helps you think about what is important to you.

A. Read the sentences. What is important to you? Check (✓) five sentences. Then rank them from 1 to 5. (Put a *1* next to the most important thing.)

what Do You Want in a Home?

- ☐ ___ I want to live in a convenient location, near stores and restaurants.
- ☐ ___ I don't want to pay a lot of rent.
- ☐ ___ I want a private room.
- ☐ ___ I want to live with my extended family.
- ☐ ___ I want to live with good friends.
- ☐ ___ I want to have nice neighbors.
- ☐ ___ I want a home near public transportation.
- ☐ ___ I want to live near a garden or park.

B. Work with a partner. Compare your answers in Activity A. Do you and your partner agree or disagree?

Listening Skill   **Listening for opinions** web⁺

CD 2
Track 4

An **opinion** is something that a person thinks or feels. Speakers sometimes use *I think (that)* when they give an opinion.

> **I think that** this house is very beautiful.   **I think** the location is very good.

Sometimes speakers give opinions with the words they choose. Listen for verbs (*like*, *love*, and *hate*), adjectives (*cheap*, *expensive*, *beautiful*, and *ugly*) or the word *only*.

> **I love** this apartment.   It's **expensive**.
> The rent is **only** $400 a month. (= I think that the rent is low.)

Listen to the conversations. What opinions do you hear? Check (✓) them.

1. Rob and Sam look at an apartment.
   - ☐ Rob and Sam like the location.
   - ☐ They think the apartment is too far from school.
   - ☐ They think that the rent is expensive.
   - ☐ They think the rent is good.

2. Mary talks to her mother.
   - ☐ Mary likes taking the bus.
   - ☐ Mary doesn't like taking the bus.
   - ☐ Mary likes her neighbors.
   - ☐ Mary doesn't like her neighbors.

3. Matt visits James's new house.
   - ☐ Matt likes James's new house.
   - ☐ Matt doesn't like James's new house.
   - ☐ James thinks that there are a lot of bedrooms.
   - ☐ James thinks that there aren't a lot of bedrooms.

4. Kate gets a new apartment.
   - ☐ Kate likes the living room in her new apartment.
   - ☐ Kate doesn't like the living room in her new apartment.
   - ☐ Mika thinks the apartment is in a good location.
   - ☐ Mika thinks the apartment is in a bad location.

LISTENING 2 | Housing Problems, Housing Solutions

VOCABULARY

Here are some words from Listening 2. Read the definitions. Then complete the sentences below.

> **affordable** (*adjective*) not expensive
>
> **condition** (*noun*) something in good condition is not damaged or broken
>
> **demand** (*noun*) a need or want
>
> **entertainment** (*noun*) fun or free-time activities
>
> **housing** (*noun*) apartments, houses, and homes
>
> **increase** (*verb*) to become bigger
>
> **landlord** (*noun*) a person—he or she rents homes to people for money
>
> **shortage** (*noun*) not enough of something

1. This house is in bad _____. There are holes in the walls, and it has two broken windows.

2. I have to talk to my _____. The lock on my front door is broken. I want him to fix it.

3. This apartment isn't _____. It's just too expensive!

4. We are having a water _____. People need to save water.

5. _____ in this area is a big problem. There aren't enough apartments or houses.

6. Rents _____ every year. I have to pay two percent more this year.

7. There is a big _____ for dormitory rooms this year. Everyone wants to live in the dorms.

8. Concerts are my favorite type of _____. I try to go to one every weekend.

PREVIEW LISTENING 2

Housing Problems, Housing Solutions

You are going to listen to Dr. Ross Chan. He is at a town meeting. He wants the city of Jackson to build more housing for students.

Read the sentences below. Check (✓) the possible problems.

☐ There are not many dormitories.

☐ Many apartments aren't affordable for students.

☐ Some cheap apartments are near entertainment, like movie theaters.

☐ Some apartments are near the campus and in safe areas.

☐ Rents are not increasing.

☐ Some inexpensive housing is in bad condition.

COMPREHENSION CHECK

 CD 2 Track 6

A. Listen to the lecture. Dr. Chan mentions three housing choices for students. What are they? Circle the correct letters.

a. Students can live in cheap apartments downtown.

b. They can live with many friends in a house.

c. The can live in cheap hotel rooms.

d. They can go to a different university.

e. They can live at home with their families.

B. Read the statements. Listen again. Write *T* (true) or *F* (false). Then correct each false statement to make it true.

___ 1. The new campus is large.

___ 2. There is a lot of entertainment downtown.

___ 3. The apartments downtown are not in good condition.

___ 4. More people want to live downtown.

___ 5. The neighborhoods near campus are safe.

___ 6. All students can live with their families.

___ 7. The new university can increase business in Jackson.

___ 8. The city doesn't want the university to grow.

the city of Jackson

 WHAT DO YOU THINK?

A. Dr. Chan mentions three options for students. Which option do you think is the best? Why? Write three reasons. Then discuss your answer with a partner.

Best option: _____

Reason 1: _____

Reason 2: _____

Reason 3: _____

B. Think about both Listening 1 and Listening 2 and discuss the questions.

1. What are the three most important things for a home?

2. What are three possible problems with a home?

> **Compound nouns** are two-word nouns. The first noun is like an adjective. It describes the second noun. You write some compounds nouns as one word and some as two words.
>
> **One word:** bathtub, streetcar, backyard
> **Two words:** shopping mall, police officer, public transportation

A. Read the sentences. Circle the compound nouns.

He parks in the driveway.

1. He parks his car in the driveway, not in the garage.

2. The apartment has three bedrooms and two bathrooms.

3. There is a swimming pool in the backyard.

4. They like to sit by the fireplace and read.

5. She doesn't have a mailbox, so she gets her mail from the post office.

6. I need to buy a smoke alarm for the living room.

7. There is a drugstore near my home.

8. There is a bookshelf in the dining room.

B. Read the definitions. Then write a compound noun from the Building Vocabulary box above or from Activity A.

Tip for Success

To make a plural compound noun, add an -s to the end of the compound noun. Don't add an -s to the first word in the noun.

Correct: *post offices*
Incorrect: *posts offices*

1. _____ People get their mail from this place.

2. _____ People put their books in this.

3. _____ This is in front of a house. You can park your car here.

4. _____ This is usually in the living room. You burn wood in it for heat.

5. _____ This is an open area behind a house. It usually has grass and trees.

6. _____ You buy medicine here.

7. _____ You can buy clothes, books, and other items here.

8. _____ This is a kind of transportation in a city.

CD 2
Track 7

In compound nouns, the stress is usually on the **first** word of the compound.

post office   **book**shelf   **drug**store

CD 2
Track 8

A. Listen to the compound nouns. The speaker will say each compound noun twice. Which pronunciation is correct? Circle *a* or *b*.

1. swimming pool   a.   b.
2. bookshelf   a.   b.
3. bedroom   a.   b.
4. shopping mall   a.   b.
5. driveway   a.   b.
6. post office   a.   b.
7. grandson   a.   b.
8. mailbox   a.   b.
9. living room   a.   b.
10. fireplace   a.   b.

swimming pool

fireplace

B. Write four sentences with the compound nouns in Activity A. Then read your sentences to a partner.

1. _____

2. _____

3. _____

4. _____

SPEAKING

Grammar **Prepositions of location** *Part 1*

Prepositions of location answer the question, "Where?"

Use *in* with countries and cities.

The Eiffel Tower is **in Paris**.

Use *on* with the names of streets and roads.

The apartment is **on Oak Street**.

Use *at* with a place in a city or a specific address.

The study group meets **at my house**.   My house is **at 333 Oak Street**.

A. Circle the correct preposition.

1. Sam is staying (in / on / at) his brother's apartment.

2. Emma lives (in / on / at) Shanghai.

3. Hassan's house is (in / on / at) Oak Street.

4. The post office is (in / on / at) 415 First Street.

5. The bank is (in / on / at) Ocean Avenue.

6. The university is (in / on / at) Miami.

B. Answer the questions with information about you. Use *in*, *on*, and *at* in your answers. Practice the questions and answers with a partner.

1. A: What country do you live in?

    B: _____.

2. A: What city do you live in?

    B: _____.

3. A: What street do you live on?

    B: _____.

4. A: What address do you live at?

    B: _____.

Look at the map and read the sentences with the prepositions of location.

The bank is **next to** the library. The library is **between** the bank and the gift shop. The gift shop is **across** (the street) **from** the bookstore. The bookstore is **on the corner of** Oak Street and Central Avenue. The parking lot is **behind** the supermarket.

A. Look at the map in the box above. Complete the sentences with prepositions of location.

1. The library is _____ the bank.

2. The gift shop is _____ Oak Street and Central Avenue.

3. The playground is _____ Jackson Park.

4. The theater is _____ the bookstore and the coffee shop.

5. The coffee shop is _____ the supermarket.

6. The parking lot is _____ the supermarket.

7. Jackson Park is _____ Oak Street and Central Avenue.

8. The bookstore is _____ the theater.

9. The bank is _____ Jackson Park.

10. The gift shop is _____ Oak Street and Central Avenue.

B. There is an error in each sentence. Find the errors and correct them.

1. My apartment building is ~~on~~ *at* 698 Pine Street.

2. The bookstore is in the corner of Central Avenue and Oak Street.

3. The library is between to the bank and the gift shop.

4. The bank is across the street to Jackson Park.

5. The playground is behind of Jackson Park.

6. The theater is next from the coffee shop.

C. Write sentences about places in your city. Use the prepositions of location.

1. (on the corner of) _____

_____

2. (across the street from) _____

_____

3. (behind)_____

_____

4. (between)_____

_____

5. (next to) _____

In this assignment, you design your perfect home and present your design to the class. As you prepare, think about the question, "What makes a good home?" and use the Self-Assessment checklist on page 92.

CONSIDER THE IDEAS

 CD 2
Track 9

Listen to the presentation. Check (✓) the ideas that the speakers give.

1. What is the inside of the house like?	
☐ four bedrooms	☐ comfortable chairs and sofas
☐ three bathrooms	☐ a big television
☐ a big kitchen	☐ a big window
☐ a big living room	

2. What is the outside of the home like?	
☐ a big backyard	☐ trees and flowers
☐ a big front yard	☐ a big driveway
☐ a table with chairs	☐ a swimming pool

3. What is the neighborhood like?	
☐ near a shopping mall	☐ near a supermarket
☐ across the street from a park	☐ quiet
☐ good public transportation	☐ nice neighbors

PREPARE AND SPEAK

A. GATHER IDEAS Work in a group of three. In your notebook, make a chart like the one in Consider the Ideas. Talk about the questions in the chart and write down your ideas. During your discussion, use expressions for giving your opinions, agreeing, and disagreeing.

Skill Review | **Agreeing and disagreeing**

Remember: During your discussion, you can agree and disagree politely using the expressions below. Review the Speaking Skill box in Unit 5, page 72.

| **Agreeing** | I do too. / Me too. | I don't either. / Me neither. |
| **Disagreeing** | Oh, I don't know. | I'm not sure. |

B. ORGANIZE IDEAS Look at your chart in Activity A. Choose the four most important items in each column. Follow these steps.

1. On a large sheet of paper, draw a map of your perfect home.
   - Draw the rooms inside the house.
   - Draw the outside of the house.
   - Show some of the neighborhood.

2. Each person chooses one part of the home to describe.

3. Practice your presentation.

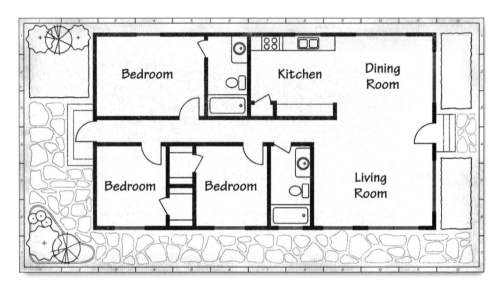

C. SPEAK Put your home drawing on the wall. Take turns presenting information about your home. Look at the Self-Assessment checklist below before you begin.

CHECK AND REFLECT

A. CHECK Think about the Unit Assignment and complete the Self-Assessment checklist.

SELF-ASSESSMENT		
Yes	No	
☐	☐	My information was clear.
☐	☐	I used vocabulary from this unit.
☐	☐	I used prepositions of location correctly.
☐	☐	I listened for the opinions of my group members.
☐	☐	I agreed and disagreed with opinions appropriately.

B. **REFLECT** Discuss these questions with a partner.

1. What is something new you learned in this unit?

2. Think about the Unit Question, "What makes a good home?" What are the main things that people want in a home?

Track Your Success

Circle the words you learned in this unit.

Nouns
backyard
bathroom 🔑
bathtub
bedroom 🔑
bookshelf
condition 🔑
demand 🔑
driveway
drugstore
entertainment 🔑
extended family
fireplace
housing
landlord
location AWL

mailbox
police officer
post office
public transportation
rent 🔑
roommate
shopping mall
shortage
smoke alarm
streetcar
swimming pool

Adjectives
affordable
comfortable 🔑
noisy 🔑
private 🔑

Verb
increase 🔑

Prepositions
across from
behind 🔑
between 🔑
near 🔑
next to
on the corner of

🔑 Oxford 2000 keywords
AWL Academic Word List

Check (✓) the skills you learned. If you need more work on a skill, refer to the page(s) in parentheses.

LISTENING	●	I can identify opinions. (p. 81)
VOCABULARY	●	I can use compound nouns. (p. 86)
GRAMMAR	●	I can use prepositions of location. (pp. 88–89)
PRONUNCIATION	●	I can pronounce compound nouns correctly. (p. 87)
SPEAKING	●	I can agree and disagree. (p. 91)
LEARNING OUTCOME	●	I can design a home and present my design to the class. (p. 91)

UNIT **7**

Weather

LISTENING ● listening for opinions
VOCABULARY ● nouns and adjectives for weather
GRAMMAR ● adverbs of frequency
PRONUNCIATION ● stressing important words
SPEAKING ● asking for repetition

Unit QUESTION

How does the weather affect you?

PREVIEW THE UNIT

Ⓐ **Which words are for weather? Circle them.
Then compare with a partner.**

rain	cold	thunder	sun	snow
lightning	beach	wind	cloud	happy
warm	hot	skiing	storm	city

Ⓑ **Look at the photo. What is the weather like?
What is happening?**

Ⓒ **Discuss the Unit Question above with your classmates.**

🔊 Listen to *The Q Classroom*, Track 10 on CD 2, to hear other answers.

LISTENING 1 | The World of Weather

VOCABULARY

Here are some words from Listening 1. Read the definitions. Then complete the sentences below.

 Tip for Success

The words *affect* and *effect* sound similar and they have a similar meaning. However, *effect* is a noun and *affect* is a verb.

> **affect** (*verb*) to make something change
>
> **cause** (*verb*) to make something happen
>
> **delay** (*noun*) a situation when something happens late
>
> **effect** (*noun*) a change that happens because of something
>
> **flood** (*noun*) a lot of water on the ground from rain
>
> **power** (*noun*) electricity we use for equipment like televisions, computers, and lights
>
> **severe** (*adjective*) very bad
>
> **temperature** (*noun*) how hot or cold something is

1. There are _____ weather conditions today. There's a lot of rain and it's extremely windy.

2. The _____ is out. The lights don't work.

3. There's a _____ in our city. There's water everywhere!

4. The _____ today is 25 degrees Celsius.

5. There's a long _____ at the airport. All the planes are late.

6. The rain isn't having any _____ on the traffic. It isn't raining very hard.

7. Snowstorms _____ terrible traffic problems every winter.

8. Hot weather doesn't really _____ me when I'm in my office. I have air conditioning, so it's nice and cool in here.

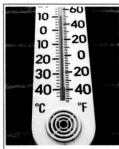

Use *degrees* to talk about temperature. You measure temperatures in *Celsius* or *Fahrenheit*.

PREVIEW LISTENING 1

The World of Weather

You are going to listen to a report about weather around the world. Talk with a partner about the weather in your city. What's the weather like today?

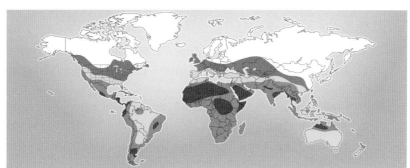

Tip for Success

Use *it's* to talk about the weather. For example, *It's sunny. It's raining. It's warm. It's cold. It's 20 degrees.*

Skill Review | **Listening for opinions**

Remember: Speakers sometimes use *I think* (*that*) when they give an opinion. Speakers also give opinions with adjectives (*nice* and *beautiful*). Review the Speaking Skill box in Unit 6, page 81.

COMPREHENSION CHECK

CD 2
Track 11

A. Look at the places in the chart. Then listen to the weather report. Check (✓) *Good weather* or *Bad weather* for each place.

Tip for Success

It's important to understand the context of information. For example, the temperatures in the weather report are in Celsius.

	Good weather	Bad weather
1. Tokyo, Japan	☐	☑
2. Beijing, China	☐	☐
3. Cairo, Egypt	☐	☐
4. Jeddah, Saudi Arabia	☐	☐
5. Paris, France	☐	☐
6. London, England	☐	☐
7. Rio de Janeiro, Brazil	☐	☐
8. Lima, Peru	☐	☐
9. New York, New York, USA	☐	☐
10. Los Angeles, California, USA	☐	☐

B. **Read the sentences. Then listen again. Circle the answer to complete each statement.**

Tip for Success

In Activity B, you answer multiple-choice questions. Always read the questions and all possible answers before you listen. This helps you focus on the important information.

1. In Beijing and Tokyo, ____.
   a. the airports have delays
   b. the airports are closed
   c. the roads are closed
   d. the trains have delays

2. In some parts of Asia, ____.
   a. there are floods in the cities
   b. there are a lot of car accidents
   c. the roads are closed
   d. people don't have power

3. In Jeddah ____.
   a. it's 45 degrees
   b. the weather is hot and windy
   c. the weather is warm and beautiful
   d. many airports are closed

4. In Paris and London, ____.
   a. it's cool and sunny
   b. it's cool and rainy
   c. it's extremely cold, but sunny
   d. it's warm and sunny

5. In Peru and Brazil, ____.
   a. the weather is the same
   b. the weather is different
   c. it's warm and rainy
   d. it's warm and beautiful

6. In Los Angeles, ____.
   a. people are outside today
   b. it's snowing
   c. it's very hot
   d. it's sunny and cold

 WHAT DO YOU THINK?

Discuss the questions with a partner.

1. What is your favorite kind of weather? Why do you like this kind of weather?

2. What kind of weather do you not like? Why not?

3. What kinds of weather cause problems for you? What problems does the weather cause?

VOCABULARY

Here are some words from Listening 2. Read the sentences. Which explanation is correct? Circle *a* or *b*.

1. Don't talk to John. He's in a bad **mood** because he failed his exam.
   a. John is feeling bad right now.
   b. John is a bad student because he didn't do well.

2. Toshi is very **cheerful** today. He got a new job and he got an A on his test.
   a. Toshi is happy.
   b. Toshi is sad.

3. It's really hot here **during** the summer. It's usually about 35 degrees Celsius in July.
   a. It's hot here in the summer.
   b. It's hot here after the summer.

4. Sarah is **depressed** today. She doesn't want to do anything.
   a. Sarah is very happy.
   b. Sarah is very unhappy.

5. Carlos is trying to choose a new city to live in. Weather is one **factor** in his choice. He likes warm weather.
   a. The weather affects Carlos's choice.
   b. Carlos doesn't care about warm weather.

6. In the winter, sunlight **decreases**. It gets dark early in the day.
   a. There is more light in the winter.
   b. There is less light in the winter.

Amanda has a headache and a cough.

7. Amanda is sick. Her **symptoms** are a headache and a cough.
   a. Amanda knows she is sick because of her headache and cough.
   b. Amanda knows she is sick so she is taking medicine.

8. Sam is **irritable** today. Don't ask him for help now. Wait until he's in a good mood.
   a. Sam is a little bit angry today.
   b. Sam is at home sick today.

PREVIEW LISTENING 2

Weather and Our Moods

You are going to listen to a lecture about how weather affects our moods. Discuss the questions with your classmates.

1. In your country, does the sunlight decrease or increase in November and December?

2. How do you feel when it's warm and sunny?

3. How do you feel when it's cloudy and rainy?

4. How do you feel when it's extremely hot or cold?

COMPREHENSION CHECK

CD 2
Track 12

A. Listen to the lecture. What kinds of weather does the speaker talk about? Check (✓) the weather.

☐ strong winds	☐ extremely hot summers	☐ cloudy skies
☐ cold, dark winters	☐ thunderstorms	☐ beautiful weather

CD 2
Track 12

B. Read the statements. Listen to the lecture again. Write *T* (true) or *F* (false) for each sentence. Then correct each false statement to make it true.

____ 1. Sunlight affects our brains.

____ 2. SAD stands for Seasonal Affective Disorder.

____ 3. People develop SAD during bright, sunny winters.

____ 4. There are only two symptoms of SAD.

____ 5. People with SAD feel sad and tired.

____ 6. People can gain weight during dark winters and very hot summers.

____ 7. Very hot weather makes people sleep a lot.

____ 8. Extremely hot weather sometimes makes people cheerful.

 **WHAT DO YOU THINK?**

A. Discuss the questions with a partner.

1. What is your favorite season? Why?

2. What is your least favorite season? Why?

B. Think about both Listening 1 and Listening 2. Read the statements. Check (✓) your answers. Then discuss your answers with a partner.

A: I really don't like hot weather.
B: Really? Why?
A: It makes me irritable.

	Strongly agree	Agree	Not sure	Disagree	Strongly disagree
Weather affects my moods.	○	○	○	○	○
I eat more in the summer.	○	○	○	○	○
I'm active in hot weather.	○	○	○	○	○
I like extremely hot weather.	○	○	○	○	○
I like cold, dark weather.	○	○	○	○	○
I sleep more in the winter.	○	○	○	○	○

Building Vocabulary | **Nouns and adjectives for weather**

There are many nouns and adjectives for weather. For many weather words, you can add -*y* to the noun to make an adjective.

Noun → Adjective

chill – chilly	fog – fog**gy**	snow – snow**y**	sun – sunn**y**
cloud – cloud**y**	rain – rain**y**	storm – storm**y**	wind – wind**y**

A. Read the sentences. Circle the correct form of the word.

1. There is a really big (cloud / cloudy) in the sky.

2. It's a (storm / stormy) day. Look at all the rain!

3. John likes (sun / sunny) weather the best.

4. You need to wear boots today. There's a lot of (snow / snowy) on the ground.

5. The (wind / windy) is strong today.

6. Anna doesn't like (rain / rainy) days.

7. They don't like to drive in (fog / foggy) weather.

8. There's a (chill / chilly) in the air.

I don't like to drive in this weather.

B. What is the weather like in your city in each season? Complete the sentences with words from Activity A. Then share your sentences with a group.

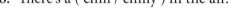

1. In the winter, it's _____.

2. In the summer, it's _____.

3. In the fall, it's _____.

4. In the spring, it's _____.

SPEAKING

1. Adverbs of frequency answer the question, "*How often?*"

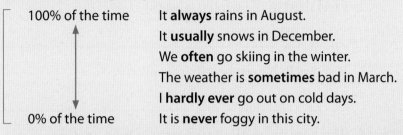

100% of the time	It **always** rains in August.
	It **usually** snows in December.
	We **often** go skiing in the winter.
	The weather is **sometimes** bad in March.
	I **hardly ever** go out on cold days.
0% of the time	It is **never** foggy in this city.

Adverbs of frequency come <u>after</u> the verb *be*.	Adverbs of frequency come <u>before</u> other verbs.
It'<u>s</u> **usually** cold in Nepal in December.	John **never** <u>wears</u> a raincoat.
We <u>are</u> **hardly ever** hot in the summer.	They **sometimes** <u>take</u> a vacation in June.

2. *Usually* and *sometimes* can also come at the <u>beginning</u> of a sentence.

Usually it's cold in Nepal in December.
Sometimes they take a vacation in June.

A. Six of the sentences have errors. The adverb of frequency is in the wrong place. Find the errors and correct them.

1. It rains (usually) in May.

2. The weather is always bad here.

3. I hear often thunder in July.

4. The winter is warm never.

5. Brazil never is cold.

6. Hardly ever we have big storms.

7. It is very cold often in Norway.

8. Sometimes it snows in the spring.

B. Write new sentences. Use the adverbs of frequency in parentheses. For some items, there is more than one correct answer.

1. It's very hot in August. (usually)

   _____

2. I feel tired in the winter. (always)

   _____

3. It snows in November. (hardly ever)

   _____

4. There are severe thunderstorms in June. (never)

   _____

5. It snows in the mountains in September. (sometimes)

   _____

 for Success

When you ask questions about frequency, you can use *ever*. The word *ever* comes before the verb.

C. Answer the questions. Write complete sentences with adverbs of frequency. Then compare your answers with a classmate.

A: Do you ever stay home in very hot weather?
B: Yes, I always stay home in very hot weather.

1. Do you ever stay home in very hot weather?

   _____

2. Do you ever feel sad when it's cold and cloudy?

   _____

3. Do you ever feel tired when it's extremely hot?

_____

4. Is your city ever extremely hot in the summer?

_____

5. Do you ever play sports in the winter?

_____

6. Does your city ever have floods?

_____

7. Does your city ever lose power during storms?

_____

Speaking Skill | **Asking for repetition**

Use these expressions to ask for repetition when you don't
understand something.

CD 2
Track 13

Excuse me?	What did you say?
A: It's hot today!	A: The weather report is on.
B: **Excuse me?**	B: Sorry. **What did you say?**
A: It's very hot today.	A: I want to listen to the weather report.
B: Yes, it is.	B: Oh, OK.

We usually use the expression _I'm sorry. Could you repeat that?_ when we ask
for information and don't understand the answer.

We often ask for repetition of **numbers** because many numbers have
similar sounds.

Could you repeat that?
A: What's the temperature today?
B: It's 13 degrees.
A: **I'm sorry. Could you repeat that?**
B: Sure. It's 13 degrees.

A. Listen to the conversations. Answer the questions.

1. What is the weather like in Seoul today?
   a. It's rainy and cloudy.
   b. It's really cold.
   c. It's really cloudy.
   d. It's sunny and chilly.

2. What's the temperature right now?
   a. It's 30 degrees.
   b. It's 13 degrees.
   c. It's 33 degrees.
   d. It's 34 degrees.

3. What is the woman's problem?
   a. There are floods in London.
   b. There are traffic delays.
   c. The trains aren't running.
   d. The airport is closed.

4. What kind of weather does the man like?
   a. He likes hot, sunny weather.
   b. He likes warm, clear weather.
   c. He likes warm, sunny weather.
   d. He likes cool, windy weather.

Tip Critical Thinking

In Activity B, you **apply** the information in this unit. You use the vocabulary, grammar, and speaking skills. This helps you remember the information better.

B. Work with a partner. Choose a city. Ask and answer these questions about the city. Ask for repetition.

A: How hot is it in the summer?
B: It's about 33 degrees.
A: Excuse me?
B: It's usually 33 degrees.

City: _____

1. What's the weather like in the summer?

2. What's the weather like in the winter?

3. How hot is it in the summer?

4. How cold is it in the winter?

5. What's your favorite season in this city? Why?

Speakers sometimes stress important words, like numbers and adverbs of frequency. Speakers use stress to:

- **answer a question**. Speakers stress the words with the answer to the question.
- **correct mistakes**. Speakers stress the word they are correcting.

**CD 2
Track 15**

Answering a question	Correcting a mistake
A: Excuse me. Where does this bus go? B: It goes **downtown**.	A: It's 13 degrees in Mexico City today. B: Excuse me? **30** degrees? A: No, **13** degrees.

**CD 2
Track 16**

A. Which words will the second speaker stress in each conversation?

- Underline the stressed words in B's answers.
- Listen to the sentences. Are your answers correct?
- Practice the conversations with a partner.

1. A: Is the airport closed?

   B: No, it's <u>open</u>.

2. A: What's the weather like in Madrid?

   B: It's very cold.

3. **A:** What kind of weather do you like?

   B: Well, I really like hot, sunny weather.

4. **A:** Do you want to go shopping?

   B: No, I don't want to go shopping. I want to go swimming.

5. **A:** Is it 14 degrees in Dubai today?

   B: No, it's 40 degrees.

B. Answer the questions with complete sentences. Then circle the stressed words in your answers.

1. What kind of weather do you like?

   _____

2. What kind of weather do you <u>not</u> like?

   _____

3. What is your favorite month of the year?

   _____

4. What's the weather like today?

   _____

5. What do you want to do this weekend?

   _____

C. Ask and answer the questions in Activity B with a partner. Ask for repetition when you don't understand something.

Unit Assignment | **Participate in a group discussion about weather**

 In this assignment, you have a group discussion about the weather. Think about the Unit Question, "How does the weather affect you?" and use the Self-Assessment checklist on page 110.

CONSIDER THE IDEAS

 A group of students is discussing the question, "How does weather affect your life?" Listen and check (✓) the sentences that you hear. Compare your answers with a partner.

- ☐ 1. I sometimes lose power in thunderstorms.
- ☐ 2. Winter has a really good effect on me.
- ☐ 3. I don't like being cold.
- ☐ 4. I hate hot weather.
- ☐ 5. I get sick every winter.
- ☐ 6. Cloudy weather makes me sad.
- ☐ 7. I don't think that weather affects me at all.
- ☐ 8. I think weather affects all of us.

PREPARE AND SPEAK

A. **GATHER IDEAS** **How does weather affect your life? Write your ideas in the chart.**

Bad effects of weather on my life	Good effects of weather on my life

B. **ORGANIZE IDEAS** Write sentences about five ideas from Activity A.

1. _____

2. _____

3. _____

4. _____

5. _____

C. **SPEAK** With a group, discuss the Unit Question, "How does weather affect you?" Look at the Self-Assessment checklist below before you begin.

- State your ideas clearly and listen for other students' ideas.
- Ask for repetition when you do not understand something.
- Stress words that give important information.

CHECK AND REFLECT

A. **CHECK** Think about the Unit Assignment and complete the Self-Assessment checklist.

Yes	No	SELF-ASSESSMENT
☐	☐	I used vocabulary from this unit.
☐	☐	I used adverbs of frequency correctly.
☐	☐	I asked for repetition when necessary in the group discussion.
☐	☐	I listened for people's opinions.
☐	☐	I used word stress correctly for important information.

B. **REFLECT** Discuss these questions with a partner.

1. What is something new you learned in this unit?

2. Think about the Unit Question, "How does the weather affect you?" What is the most important way that weather affects your life?

Track Your Success

Circle the words you learned in this unit.

Nouns	Adjectives	Adverbs
degree 🔑	cheerful	always 🔑
delay	chilly	hardly ever
effect 🔑	cloudy	never 🔑
factor **AWL**	depressed **AWL**	sometimes 🔑
flood 🔑	foggy	usually 🔑
mood 🔑	irritable	**Preposition**
power 🔑	rainy	during 🔑
symptom	severe	
temperature 🔑	snowy	
	stormy	
Verbs	sunny	
affect 🔑 **AWL**	windy	
cause 🔑		
decrease		

🔑 Oxford 2000 keywords

AWL Academic Word List

Check (✓) the skills you learned. If you need more work on a skill, refer to the page(s) in parentheses.

LISTENING	●	I can identify opinions. (p. 97)
VOCABULARY	●	I can understand many nouns and adjectives for weather. (p. 101)
GRAMMAR	●	I can use adverbs of frequency. (p. 103)
PRONUNCIATION	●	I can stress important words in a sentence. (p. 107)
SPEAKING	●	I can ask for repetition. (p. 105)
LEARNING OUTCOME	●	I can participate in a group discussion about weather. (p. 108)

UNIT 8

Health

LISTENING ● listening for frequency
VOCABULARY ● adjectives ending in -ed
GRAMMAR ● modals can and should
PRONUNCIATION ● can, can't, should, and shouldn't
SPEAKING ● asking for repetition

LEARNING OUTCOME

Create, conduct, and discuss a health survey.

Unit QUESTION

What do you do to stay healthy?

PREVIEW THE UNIT

A Check (✓) the statements that are true for you. Then compare with a partner. How do you think these things affect your health?

- ☐ I eat a lot of sweets and desserts.
- ☐ I spend a lot of time with friends.
- ☐ I exercise a lot.
- ☐ I watch television every day.
- ☐ I often play video games.
- ☐ I am on a sports team.
- ☐ I drink a lot of water.
- ☐ I worry a lot.

B Look at the photo. Where is the man? Where is he going?

C Discuss the Unit Question above with your classmates.

🔊 Listen to *The Q Classroom*, Track 18 on CD 2, to hear other answers.

113

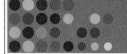

LISTENING

LISTENING 1 | Health Watch

VOCABULARY

Here are some words from Listening 1. Read the definitions. Then complete the sentences below.

> **diet** (*noun*) the food that you usually eat
>
> **energy** (*noun*) the ability to be active and not become tired
>
> **lonely** (*adjective*) sad because you are not with other people
>
> **manage** (*verb*) to control something
>
> **reduce** (*verb*) to make something smaller
>
> **run-down** (*adjective*) very tired and not healthy, often because you are working too hard
>
> **stress** (*noun*) a feeling of being very worried because of problems in your life
>
> **stressful** (*adjective*) causing stress

1. Toshi is sad because he feels _____. He doesn't have many friends in his new city.

2. Kate works 60 hours a week. She wants to _____ her time at work to 40 hours a week.

3. Mary is feeling a lot of _____ right now. She has three exams this week!

4. I don't have any _____. I feel tired all the time.

5. Sam has an unhealthy _____. He has pizza and soda for lunch every day. He hardly ever eats vegetables.

6. This is a _____ time. I have two tests and I'm sick.

7. Anna doesn't _____ her schedule very well. She's always late and she often forgets to do her homework.

8. David is working two jobs and taking four classes. He looks really _____.

pizza and soda

PREVIEW LISTENING 1

Health Watch

You are going to listen to a podcast interview with Dr. Michael Smith about stress. When do people feel stress? Check (✓) your answers and add one more idea.

People can feel stress when . . . .

- ☐ they have money problems
- ☐ they get together with friends
- ☐ they exercise a lot
- ☐ they work long hours
- ☐ they want good grades
- ☐ they have healthy diets
- ☐ they are lonely
- ☐ _____

COMPREHENSION CHECK

 CD 2
Track 19

A. Listen to the podcast. What ideas and topics does the podcast mention? Circle the ideas and topics.

vacations	money	sickness	music	coffee
(work)	rent	headaches	exercise	friends
children	grades	sleep	food	medicine

B. Read the sentences in the chart. Then listen again. Check (✓) the correct column for each sentence.

	Causes of stress	Symptoms of stress	Ways to reduce stress
1. People feel run-down.	☐	✓	☐
2. They exercise.	☐	☐	☐
3. They worry about money.	☐	☐	☐
4. They have a good diet.	☐	☐	☐
5. They're very busy.	☐	☐	☐
6. They don't have energy.	☐	☐	☐
7. They feel lonely.	☐	☐	☐
8. They have social time.	☐	☐	☐
9. They gain weight.	☐	☐	☐
10. They worry about grades.	☐	☐	☐

Tip for Success

In Unit 7, you learned the verb *cause* (to make something happen). Here, you see the noun form of *cause* (a thing that makes something happen).

Q WHAT DO YOU THINK?

When do you feel stress? Add one idea to the chart. Check (✓) your answers. Then discuss your answers with a partner.

	A lot of stress	A little stress	Not any stress
With my family	☐	☐	☐
At school	☐	☐	☐
With my neighbors	☐	☐	☐
At work	☐	☐	☐
With my friends	☐	☐	☐
_____	☐	☐	☐

A: *I don't feel any stress with my family. I have a lot of fun with my family. How about you?*

B: *I don't feel any stress with my family, but I feel a lot of stress at school.*

Frequency means "How often?" When you listen, try to hear these frequency adverbs and expressions.

Adverbs of frequency	always, usually, often, sometimes, hardly ever, never
Expressions with *every*	**every** day, **every** week, **every** year
Other expressions	**once a** week, **twice a** month, three **times a** year eight **hours a** day, four **hours** a week

CD 2
Track 20

A: Do you **always** exercise at the gym?
B: No, **sometimes** I jog in the park.
A: How often do you exercise?
B: **Three times a week.**

CD 2
Track 21

A. Listen to eight parts of a conversation. Circle the words and expressions you hear. (Three items have two answers.)

1. always   sometimes   every week

2. never   every day   once a week

3. twice a week   never   sometimes

4. six days a week   twice a week   every day

5. always   sometimes   three times a week

6. once a week   usually   twice a week

7. usually   once a day   always

8. every week   once a day   three times a week

CD 2
Track 22

B. Read the questions. Listen to the whole conversation. Circle the correct answers.

1. How many days a week does John work?
   a. five   b. six   c. seven

2. How often does John exercise?
   a. every day   b. twice a week   c. never

3. How often does Anna exercise?
   a. three days a week   b. six days a week   c. every day

4. How often does Anna go running?
   a. twice a week   b. three times a week   c. once a week

5. How often does John drink coffee with his meals?
   a. sometimes   b. always   c. usually

C. Ask and answer these questions with a partner. Listen and write your partner's answers.

A: How many times a week do you exercise?
B: Four times a week.

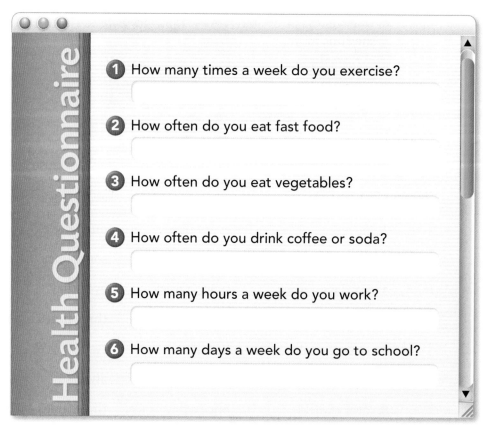

Health Questionnaire

1. How many times a week do you exercise?

2. How often do you eat fast food?

3. How often do you eat vegetables?

4. How often do you drink coffee or soda?

5. How many hours a week do you work?

6. How many days a week do you go to school?

| # How Often Do You Work Out?

VOCABULARY

Here are some words from Listening 2. Read the sentences. Which explanation is correct? Circle *a* or *b*.

1. Emma has good exercise **habits**. She works out five days a week.
   a. Emma exercises very often.
   b. Emma has nice exercise clothes.

2. John likes to **stay in shape**. He goes to the gym almost every day.
   a. John spends a lot of time indoors.
   b. John takes care of his body and health.

3. Toshi wants to **prepare** dinner for us. He is an excellent cook.
   a. Toshi wants to go out for dinner.
   b. Toshi wants to make dinner.

4. Mika goes to the gym **regularly**. She works out every evening after work.
   a. Mika exercises very often.
   b. Mika doesn't exercise every week.

5. Isabel goes running **at least** three times a week. If she has time, she runs more.
   a. Isabel sometimes runs only twice a week.
   b. Isabel sometimes runs four times a week.

6. I **watch what I eat**. For example, I don't eat food with a lot of fat or sugar.
   a. The speaker chooses her food carefully.
   b. The speaker chooses cheap and convenient food.

7. Amanda sells houses **for a living**. She works five days a week.
   a. Amanda sells houses as a job.
   b. Amanda's house is too big. She wants to sell it.

8. I started exercising last month, and I want to **keep** it **up**. I feel a lot better.
   a. The speaker wants to continue exercising this month.
   b. The speaker wants to stop exercising this month.

I started exercising.

PREVIEW LISTENING 2

How Often Do You Work Out?

You are going to listen to a reporter interview three people at a gym about their health habits.

What do people with good health habits do? What do people with bad health habits do? Write ideas in the chart. Then compare with a partner.

Tip Critical Thinking

In the Preview activity, you **compare** the actions of people with good health habits and people with bad health habits. Comparing two things is a way to understand material more deeply.

People with good health habits	People with bad health habits . . . .
watch what they eat	eat junk food

COMPREHENSION CHECK

 CD 2 Track 23

A. Listen to the interviews with Matt, Kate, and Rob. Match each person with the correct description.

1. Matt ____   a. is a lawyer.

2. Kate ____   b. is a manager at a store.

3. Rob ____   c. is a history teacher.

CD 2 Track 23

B. Look at the chart. Then listen again. Check (✓) the correct information for each person. (You will check more than one column.)

	Sleeps at least eight hours a night	Exercises at least three times a week	Doesn't work too much	Eats healthy food
1. Matt	☐	☑	☐	☐
2. Kate	☐	☐	☐	☐
3. Rob	☐	☐	☐	☐

Q WHAT DO YOU THINK?

A. Make true statements about your health habits. Circle your answers and add your own idea. Then check (✓) your good habits.

Good Habits

I watch what I eat.

1. I **exercise / don't exercise** regularly. ☐

2. I **eat / don't eat** fresh fruits and vegetables. ☐

3. I **eat / don't eat** junk food a lot. ☐

4. I **sleep / don't sleep** at least eight hours a night. ☐

5. I **work / don't work** too much. ☐

6. I **watch / don't watch** what I eat. ☐

7. I **do / don't do** relaxing activities. ☐

8. Your idea: _____ ☐

B. Think about both Listening 1 and Listening 2. What are your healthy habits? What are your unhealthy habits? Tell a partner.

Building Vocabulary   Adjectives ending in *-ed*

Tip for Success

Adjectives ending in *-ed* look like past tense verbs. A verb usually comes after a noun or subject pronoun. (*Anna **surprised** us*.) An adjective usually comes after a form of *be*. (*Anna is **surprised**.*)

Many adjectives end with *-ed*. These adjectives come from verbs. They usually describe a feeling or an emotion.

| **Verbs** | John <u>worries</u> a lot. | Anna likes to <u>relax</u> at the park. |
| **Adjectives** | John is **worried**. | Anna is **relaxed**. |

Here are some other adjectives ending with *-ed*.

bored   confused   excited   interested   relaxed   surprised   tired

A. Read the sentences. Complete each sentence with the adjective form of the word in bold.

1. Mary **worries** about school. She is always _____.

2. Soccer games **excite** James. He is _____ to play soccer today.

3. Running doesn't **interest** me. I'm not _____ in running.

4. Sam **relaxes** on the weekends. On Saturdays, he is usually _____.

5. These questions **confuse** me. I'm _____.

B. Complete each conversation with a word from the box. Then practice the conversations with a partner. You won't use all of the words.

bored	excited	interested	relaxed	surprised	tired	worried

1. **A:** What's wrong?

   B: Oh, I'm a little _____. I stayed awake really late last night.

2. **A:** I'm _____. Let's do something fun.

   B: Do you want to play tennis?

3. **A:** Guess what! My brother wants to go to the gym with us tomorrow!

   B: Wow, I'm _____! He hates exercising!

4. **A:** I'm _____ about the final exam. This class is really difficult for me.

   B: I plan to study with Isabel and Emma tonight. You can join us. Are you _____?

   A: Yes, I am! Thanks!

SPEAKING

1. A modal comes before a base form verb. Modals can be affirmative or negative.*

   I **should eat** more fruit.
      modal base verb

   I **can't sleep** some nights.
      modal base verb

   Don't put an *-s* at the end of the verb.

   ✓ Correct: He **can play** tennis well.   ✗ Incorrect: He **can plays** tennis well.

2. Use ***can/can't*** to talk about possibility or ability.

   Stress **can make** people gain weight.   Rob **can't swim**.

3. Use ***should/shouldn't*** to give advice.

   You **should exercise** every day.   You **shouldn't worry** all the time.

   *The full forms of *shouldn't* and *can't* are *should not* and *cannot*.

A. **Complete the conversation with *can*, *can't*, *should*, and *shouldn't*.
Then practice with a partner.**

Emma and Isabel

Emma: I'm worried about Kate. She looks really tired. She works too much.

Isabel: I know. She _____ work so much.
                          1

Emma: You're right. She _____ sleep more, too. She sleeps
                              2
about four hours a night! And she doesn't exercise.

Isabel: She _____ come to the gym with me. There's a great
                    3
swimming pool there.

Emma: Well, she _____ swim, but she wants to learn.
                     4
Does your gym have swimming lessons?

Isabel: Yes, it does. She _____ take lessons in the evenings or
                     5
on the weekends.

Emma: Oh, good. You _____ call her and tell her that.
                     6
I _____ come, too. I need to learn how to swim.
   7

Isabel: Yes, that's a great idea!

B. Write five sentences about stress in your life and your bad habits. (Look at the information your wrote in the *What Do You Think?* Activities on pages 116 and 121.)

I feel a lot of stress because I worry about grades.
I don't exercise regularly.
I can't sleep at night.

1. _____

2. _____

3. _____

4. _____

5. _____

C. Take turns reading your sentences with a partner. Give your partner advice. Use *should* and *shouldn't*.

A: I feel a lot of stress because I worry about grades.
B: Hmm. You should . . .

Pronunciation	*Can, can't, should,* and *shouldn't*	web

Can **and** *can't*

You do not usually stress *can* in an affirmative statement. The vowel sound is short. *Can't* is usually stressed, and the vowel sounds like *ant*. You don't pronounce the *t* clearly.

CD 2
Track 24

| She **can** swim. | She **can't** swim. |
| He **can** speak English. | He **can't** speak English. |

Should **and** *shouldn't*

Should has one syllable. *Shouldn't* has two syllables. In a sentence, you don't pronounce the *t* clearly.

| He **should** sleep more. | He **shouldn't** eat so much. |
| She **should** exercise more. | She **shouldn't** work so much. |

A. Listen to the sentences. Circle the modal that you hear.

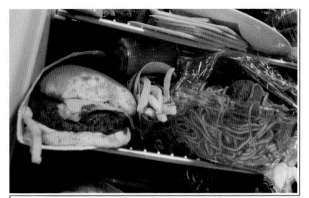

You shouldn't eat that.

1. You (should / shouldn't) eat that.

2. John (should / shouldn't) get together with his friends tonight.

3. He (can / can't) play soccer very well.

4. She (can / can't) swim.

5. Kate (can / can't) drive a car.

6. I (should / shouldn't) go to the gym in the mornings!

7. You (should / shouldn't) go to work today.

8. I (can / can't) go away this weekend.

9. We (should / shouldn't) go to that restaurant.

10. Carlos (can / can't) ride a bike.

B. Work with a partner. Take turns saying the sentences in Activity A.

C. Write six sentences about your health habits with *can*, *can't*, *should*, and *shouldn't*. Use each modal at least once.

1. _____

2. _____

3. _____

4. _____

5. _____

6. _____

D. Read your sentences from Activity C to a partner. For each of your partner's sentences, circle the modal you hear.

1. can   can't   should   shouldn't

2. can   can't   should   shouldn't

3. can   can't   should   shouldn't

4. can   can't   should   shouldn't

5. can   can't   should   shouldn't

6. can   can't   should   shouldn't

Unit Assignment | Create, conduct, and discuss a health survey

In this assignment, you create and conduct a health survey. Then you discuss the results of the survey. As you prepare, think about the Unit Question, "What do you do to stay healthy?" and use the Self-Assessment checklist on page 128.

CONSIDER THE IDEAS

CD 2
Track 26

A. Listen to the students discuss their sample survey. Check (✓) the questions that you hear.

☐ 1. How many hours do you work every week?
☐ 2. How many hours do you sleep every night?
☐ 3. How often do you exercise?
☐ 4. What do you do with your friends?
☐ 5. What do you do to relax?

PREPARE AND SPEAK

A. **GATHER IDEAS** Work with a partner. Write six questions about health habits. Include questions about diet, sleep, and work.

1. _____

2. _____

3. _____

4. _____

5. _____

6. _____

B. **ORGANIZE IDEAS** With your partner, look at your health questions from Activity A. Choose the three best questions and write them in the survey form.

Question 1 _____

Student 1 _____
_____

Student 2 _____
_____

Student 3 _____
_____

Question 2 _____

Student 1 _____
_____

Student 2 _____
_____

Student 3 _____
_____

Question 3 _____

Student 1 _____
_____

Student 2 _____
_____

Student 3 _____
_____

Remember: Ask for repetition when you do not understand something. Use the expressions below. Review the Speaking Skill box in Unit 7, page 105.

> Excuse me?
> Sorry, what did you say?
> I'm sorry. Could you repeat that?

C. **SPEAK** Follow these steps. Look at the Self-Assessment checklist below before you begin.

- Work individually. Ask three students your questions. Write their answers on the survey form in Activity B. You and your partner should talk to different people.

- Share your survey answers with your partner. Discuss your survey results.

A: Let's look at the first question. One person sleeps ten hours every night.

B: Three people sleep eight hours every night.

CHECK AND REFLECT

A. **CHECK** Think about the Unit Assignment and complete the Self-Assessment checklist.

SELF-ASSESSMENT		
Yes	No	
☐	☐	My information was clear.
☐	☐	I used vocabulary from this unit.
☐	☐	I used the modals *can*, *can't*, *should*, and *shouldn't* correctly.
☐	☐	I used adjectives ending with *-ed* correctly.
☐	☐	I listened for frequency expressions.

B. **REFLECT** Discuss these questions with a partner.

1. What is something new you learned in this unit?

2. Think about the Unit Question, "What do you do to stay healthy?" What are the most important things you do to stay healthy?

Track Your Success

Circle the words you learned in this unit.

Nouns
cause 🔑
diet
energy 🔑 AWL
habit 🔑
stress 🔑 AWL

Verbs
keep (something) up
manage 🔑
prepare 🔑
reduce 🔑

Adjectives
bored 🔑
confused 🔑
excited 🔑
interested 🔑
lonely 🔑
relaxed 🔑 AWL
run-down
stressful AWL
surprised 🔑
tired 🔑

Adverbs
at least 🔑
regularly 🔑

Phrases
for a living
stay in shape
watch what (I) eat

🔑 Oxford 2000 keywords
AWL Academic Word List

Check (✓) the skills you learned. If you need more work on a skill, refer to the page(s) in parentheses.

LISTENING	●	I can identify frequency words and expressions. (p. 117)
VOCABULARY	●	I can understand some adjectives ending in *-ed*. (p. 121)
GRAMMAR	●	I can use the modals *can* and *should*. (p. 123)
PRONUNCIATION	●	I can pronounce the modals *can*, *can't*, *should*, and *shouldn't*. (p. 124)
SPEAKING	●	I can ask for repetition. (p. 128)
LEARNING OUTCOME	●	I can create, conduct, and discuss a health survey. (p. 126)

Give a presentation about a special city using the simple present and simple past.

?

Unit QUESTION

What makes a city special?

PREVIEW THE UNIT

A List three special places and activities in your area. Then discuss the questions with a partner.

Special Places and Activities _____

_____

_____

1. What's your favorite place? Why?

2. What's your favorite activity? Why?

B Look at the photo. What do you see? What is special about this city?

C Discuss the Unit Question above with your classmates.

)) Listen to *The Q Classroom*, Track 27 on CD 2, to hear other answers.

LISTENING

LISTENING 1 | Travel Talk

VOCABULARY

Here are some words from Listening 1. Read the sentences. Which explanation is correct? Circle *a* or *b*.

1. In the summer, the **climate** of Tunisia is hot and dry.
   a. The weather is hot and dry in Tunisia in the summer.
   b. The beaches of Tunisia are hot and dry in the summer.

2. The **average** tourist stays at this hotel for one week, but Anna really likes it here. She is staying two weeks.
   a. Anna is like most tourists at the hotel.
   b. Anna is not like most tourists at the hotel.

3. Many tourists visit Kyoto because it is a center for Japanese **culture**. They go to Kyoto to have good Japanese food, visit museums, and see beautiful old buildings.
   a. You can learn a lot about Japanese customs and art in Kyoto.
   b. You can do a lot of shopping in Kyoto.

4. You can walk through the gardens at the park. You can also see **performances** there. You can watch plays, listen to music, and see dancers.
   a. A concert is a kind of performance.
   b. A garden is a kind of performance.

5. Mary **recently** visited Russia. She was there last month.
   a. Mary visited Russia a short time ago.
   b. Mary visited Russia a long time ago.

6. The **architecture** in Shanghai, China, is amazing! I really like the Oriental Pearl Tower and the Shanghai World Financial Center.
   a. The buildings in Shanghai are interesting.
   b. The parks in Shanghai are interesting.

Oriental Pearl Tower

the Coliseum

7. Rome has several **historic** buildings. For example, the famous Coliseum is in Rome. It is about 2,000 years old.

   a. Rome has many important new buildings.

   b. Rome has many important old buildings.

8. Rio de Janeiro has many **skyscrapers**. One of them is Ventura Corporate Towers. It has 38 floors. Some skyscrapers have more than 40 floors.

   a. There are a lot of big offices in Rio.

   b. There are a lot of tall buildings in Rio.

PREVIEW LISTENING 1

| Travel Talk

You are going to listen to a radio program about three special cities. Look at the pictures. Match each description with the correct picture. Write the letters.

1. ____   2. ____   3. ____

a. Ubud is on an island in Bali.

b. Bruges is a historic city in Belgium.

c. New York City is a busy city in the United States.

COMPREHENSION CHECK

 CD 2 Track 28

A. Listen to the program. The interviewer talks to three people. Match each person with the correct city. (You will not use one of the names.)

1. Sam ____   a. Bruges

2. David ____   b. Ubud

3. Amanda ____   c. New York City

4. Mika ____

Remember: Frequency means "How often?" When you listen, try to hear frequency adverbs and expressions like *usually* and *every night*. Review the Listening Skill box in Unit 8, page 117.

CD 2
Track 28

B. Read the sentences. Then listen to the radio program again. Circle the answer to complete each statement.

1. The average temperature in Bali is ___.
   a. cool   b. very warm   c. very hot

2. The speaker enjoyed concerts and dance performances ___.
   a. every night   b. every weekend   c. every week

3. According to the speaker, Bruges has ___.
   a. amazing architecture   b. a big shopping mall   c. skyscrapers

4. The speaker thinks Bruges ___ in the world.
   a. is the best place   b. has the best chocolate   c. has the best food

5. The speaker visited New York ___.
   a. last week   b. last month   c. last year

6. One of the speaker's favorite things about New York is ___.
   a. the people   b. the shopping   c. the museums

Q WHAT DO YOU THINK?

A. Work with a partner. Choose a city that you both know. Complete the chart individually.

City:	Not good	OK	Good
1. culture	☐	☐	☐
2. architecture	☐	☐	☐
3. weather	☐	☐	☐
4. shopping	☐	☐	☐
5. food	☐	☐	☐

B. Discuss your chart with your partner. Give reasons for your answers.

A: I think the culture in Tokyo is good.

B: I agree. You can see a lot of dance performances there.

a street festival in Tokyo

LISTENING 2 | Making Positive Changes

VOCABULARY

Here are some words from Listening 2. Read the sentences. Then write each bold word next to the correct definition.

1. I'm not a **resident** of this city, so I can't borrow books from this library. I can only borrow books from my city's library.

2. The City leaders want to **improve** public transportation. They plan to buy twenty buses and ten trains this year.

3. The Eiffel Tower in Paris is my favorite **monument**. I also like the Taj Mahal in India.

4. This city has so many interesting **sights**. Let's go to the Modern Art Museum this afternoon and the night market this evening.

5. Go to the top of the Empire State Building at night. The **view** of the city is beautiful.

6. The City leaders want more art in the park. They asked artists to **create** new sculptures.

7. Flights to Bangkok are really cheap right now. Let's buy tickets. It's a great **opportunity**!

8. The park has a **variety** of activities. We can hike, play basketball, or ride bikes.

the Taj Mahal

a. _____ (*noun*) interesting places in a city or town—tourists like to visit them

b. _____ (*verb*) to make something better

c. _____ (*noun*) all the things you can see from a place

d. _____ (*noun*) a large sculpture or building—it helps people remember a person or event from the past

e. _____ (*noun*) a lot of different things

f. _____ (*verb*) to make something

g. _____ (*noun*) a person—he or she lives in a city, neighborhood, or building

h. _____ (*noun*) a chance to do something

PREVIEW LISTENING 2

| Making Positive Changes

You are going to hear the mayor of Seacliff give a speech about changes in the town during the past year. Look at the photo. Circle the correct words in the sentences.

1. These people are (visitors / residents).

2. They are (at city hall / in a classroom).

COMPREHENSION CHECK

CD 2
Track 29 **A.** Listen to the speech. Check (✓) the correct problem and solution for each place. (You will not check all the items.)

Problems	Parks and beaches	Historic buildings and monuments	Downtown area
1. They were dirty.	☑	☐	☐
2. They were not safe.	☐	☐	☐
3. They were in bad condition.	☐	☐	☐
4. The shops and restaurants were old.	☐	☐	☐
5. Business was bad.	☐	☐	☐
Solutions			
6. Volunteers cleaned the areas.	☐	☐	☐
7. The city hired more police.	☐	☐	☐
8. Residents gave the city money.	☐	☐	☐
9. The city built a new hospital.	☐	☐	☐
10. New shops and restaurants opened.	☐	☐	☐

B. Read the sentences. Then listen again. Circle the correct words to complete the sentences.

1. Seacliff is a (busy / quiet) city.

2. Many years ago, (a lot of tourists / no tourists) visited Seacliff.

3. The city started having problems because of (money / a bad mayor).

4. One historic building in the city is (the hospital / city hall).

5. There is a sculpture of (the first mayor / the first doctor) of Seacliff.

6. A lot of the downtown shops closed (last year / a few years ago).

7. Seacliff has a new (theater / hotel).

8. There are more (residents / jobs) in Seacliff now.

 WHAT DO YOU THINK?

A. Discuss these questions in a group.

1. Do you think Seacliff is a nice place to visit? Why or why not?

2. Is Seacliff a nice place to live? Why or why not?

 **Critical Thinking**

In Activity B, you **combine** information from Listening 1 and 2. Combining is putting ideas together. This shows you can use information in new ways.

B. Think about both Listening 1 and Listening 2. What does a city need to be special? Check (✓) five things. Number them from 1 (most important) to 5 (least important). Then compare your answers with a partner.

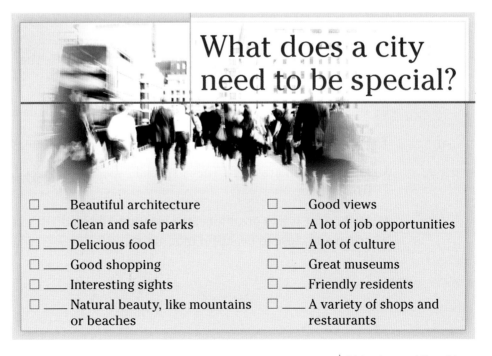

What does a city need to be special?

☐ ___ Beautiful architecture

☐ ___ Clean and safe parks

☐ ___ Delicious food

☐ ___ Good shopping

☐ ___ Interesting sights

☐ ___ Natural beauty, like mountains or beaches

☐ ___ Good views

☐ ___ A lot of job opportunities

☐ ___ A lot of culture

☐ ___ Great museums

☐ ___ Friendly residents

☐ ___ A variety of shops and restaurants

Word families are groups of similar words. Word families can include nouns, verbs, adjectives, and adverbs. For example, look at the related forms of this word:

Verb: correct
Adjective: correct
Noun: correction
Adverb: correctly

When you look up a word in the dictionary, look for other forms of the word. You can find other word forms in, above, and below the definition. For example, look at the different words forms in, above, and below *locate* and *special*.

---

lo·cate AWL /ˈloʊkeɪt/ *verb* (lo·cates, lo·cat·ing, lo·cat·ed)
to find the exact position of someone or something: *Rescue helicopters are trying to locate the missing sailors.*
▸ **lo·cat·ed** AWL /ˈloʊkeɪṭəd/ *adjective*
in a place: *The factory is located near the river.*

lo·ca·tion AWL /loʊˈkeɪʃn/ *noun* [count]
a place: *The house is in a quiet location at the top of a hill.*

---

spe·cial[1] /ˈspɛʃl/ *adjective*
1 not usual or ordinary; important for a reason: *It's my birthday today, so we're having a special dinner.*
2 for a particular person or thing: *He goes to a special school for deaf children.*

spe·cial·ize /ˈspɛʃl·aɪz/ *verb* (spe·cial·iz·es, spe·cial·iz·ing, spe·cial·ized)
specialize in something to study or know a lot about one subject, type of product, etc.: *He specialized in criminal law.*

spe·cial·ly /ˈspɛʃl·i/ *adverb*
for a particular purpose or reason: *These dogs have been specially trained to find illegal drugs.* ◆ *a specially designed chair*

All dictionary entries are from the *Oxford Basic American Dictionary for learners of English.* © Oxford University Press 2011.

A. For each sentence, circle the correct word form. Use the definitions above.

1. This is (special / specially / specialize) food from Thailand. It's sweet.

2. We can't find Khalid. We are trying to (locate / location / located) him.

3. John and Sam are chefs. They (special / specially / specialize) in food from Turkey.

4. Melbourne is in a great (locate / location / located). It's next to the ocean and close to beautiful mountains.

5. My parents cooked me a (special / specially / specialize) meal for my birthday.

6. The museum is (locate / location / located) near city hall.

7. Our lunch is (special / specially / specialize) prepared. The chef cooked it just for us!

B. Write the part of speech for each word. Then complete the sentences with the words. Use your dictionary to help you.

a. architect _____

b. architecture _____

c. perform _____

d. performance _____

e. recent _____

f. recently _____

g. variety _____

h. various _____

Matt designs buildings.

The restaurants in Bangkok were all great.

1. Matt designs buildings. He is a(n) _____.

2. In Cairo, we visited a(n) _____ of monuments.

3. Toshi _____ returned from Tokyo.

4. We loved the dance _____ in Madrid last week.

5. I tried _____ restaurants in Bangkok, and they were all great.

6. I want to study the _____ in Istanbul. The buildings there are beautiful.

7. Mary is a wonderful violinist. She wants to _____ in concerts.

8. I met Carlos on my _____ trip to Rio.

SPEAKING

| Grammar | Past of *be*; Simple past affirmative statements | |

Past of *be*

Use the past of *be* to identify and describe people and things in the past.

Affirmative and negative statements

subject	be	(not)	
I	**was**		very happy.
You We They	**were**	**(not)**	busy yesterday.
He She It	**was**		in Ubud last week.

- You can contract negative statements:

  was not = wasn't   were not = weren't

- Past time expressions answer the question, "*When?*"

  last + time: last week, last month

  time + **ago**:   three days **ago**, one year **ago**

Yes/No questions			Short answers	
be	subject		*yes*	*no*
Was	he	in China?	Yes, he **was**.	No, he **wasn't**.
Were	they	excited?	Yes, they **were**.	No, they **weren't**.

Information questions			Answers
wh- word	*be*	subject	
How	**were**	Paris and Rome?	They **were** great!
What	**was**	your favorite city?	Istanbul **was** my favorite city.
When	**was**	the concert?	The concert **was** last week.

Simple past affirmative statements

The simple past describes completed actions in the past.

Regular past verbs end in *-ed*. The simple past form is the same for all subjects.

> I **visited** Brazil last year.
> They **liked** their trip to Tokyo.
> He **shopped** downtown yesterday.
> We **stayed** at a nice hotel.

For spelling rules, see page 182.		
like-lik**ed**	stay-stay**ed**	try-tr**ied**
shop-shop**ped**	travel-travel**ed**	visit-visit**ed**

A. Put the words in the correct order. Use the correct form of *be* in each sentence. Then ask and answer the questions with a partner.

1. you / where / yesterday / be ?

   _____

2. last week / be / you / on vacation ?

   _____

3. be / last trip / how / your ?

   _____

4. last vacation / it / be / on / your / cold ?

   _____

5. be / when you were young / what / your favorite city ?

   _____

6. in this city / you / be / last year ?

   _____

B. Complete Anna's email about her trip to Istanbul. Use the past form of the words in the box.

shop	stay	travel	try	visit	walk

From: annatwo@email.org
To: sarahfive@email.org
Subject: my trip to Istanbul

I'm back from my vacation! I _____ to Istanbul last
month. My trip was so much fun! I _____ in a really nice
hotel. There was a view of a beautiful square outside my window.
During the days, I _____ a lot of great museums. I also
_____ around the city a lot.
There are so many interesting sights
and monuments in Istanbul. My feet
were tired! The food was delicious. I
_____ baklava for the first
time. It's a dessert made with nuts and
syrup. On my last day, I _____
at a big market. There were so many
pretty scarves, shoes, and bags. Let's get
together soon. I have a gift for you!

the Grand Bazaar in Istanbul

C. Write about a city you visited. Complete the sentences. Then read
your sentences to a partner.

1. I traveled to _____.

2. I visited _____.

3. I tried _____.

4. I loved _____.

5. I stayed _____.

6. There was/were _____.

There are three ways to pronounce the *-ed* of a simple past verb.

CD 2
Track 30

/t/		/d/		/ɪd/	
walk**ed**	lik**ed**	travel**ed**	lov**ed**	visit**ed**	want**ed**

CD 2
Track 31

A. Listen to the sentences. Circle the sound that you hear at the end of the verb. Then practice the sentences with a partner.

They collected shells.

1. They collected shells on the beach in Oman.   /t/   /d/   /ɪd/

2. We tried to go to the Modern Art Museum.   /t/   /d/   /ɪd/

3. He shopped all afternoon.   /t/   /d/   /ɪd/

4. We started our tour at noon.   /t/   /d/   /ɪd/

5. I worked in Dubai last year.   /t/   /d/   /ɪd/

6. Heavy traffic caused problems in Los Angeles.   /t/   /d/   /ɪd/

B. Write six sentences about a special city. Use verbs from the box.

enjoyed	needed	shopped	stayed	visited
liked	relaxed	started	tried	wanted

1. _____

2. _____

3. _____

4. _____

5. _____

6. _____

C. Read your sentences from Activity B to a partner. For each of your partner's sentences, circle the sound you hear in the chart.

1. /t/   /d/   /ɪd/ | **3.** /t/   /d/   /ɪd/ | **5.** /t/   /d/   /ɪd/

2. /t/   /d/   /ɪd/ | **4.** /t/   /d/   /ɪd/ | **6.** /t/   /d/   /ɪd/

Look at the two conversations below. In Conversation 1, Isabel asks a **closed question** (a *yes/no* question), and Sun-Hee answers "Yes." In Conversation 2, Isabel asks an **open question** (a *wh-* question). Sun Hee gives her more information. Open questions make a conversation more interesting.

CD 2
Track 32

Conversation 1: Closed question	Conversation 2: Open question
A: I visited Hong Kong last week.	**A:** I visited Hong Kong last week.
B: Was it fun?	**B: How was it?**
A: Yes.	**A:** It was great. I visited a lot of interesting sights and I tried new food.

CD 2
Track 33

A. Listen to the conversation. Complete the questions. Then practice with a partner.

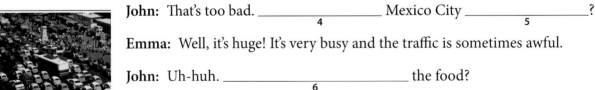

Emma: John, _____ Greece?
1

John: Fantastic! I liked Athens a lot. The museums and architecture were

    great. And the view from the top of the Acropolis was amazing!

Emma: _____?
2

John: Well, Greeks eat a lot of bread, cheese, olives, and vegetables. For

    meat, they eat a lot of lamb. I love all of those foods, so I was very happy!

Emma: That sounds great, John.

John: _____ your trip to Mexico City?
3

Emma: It was good, but I was really busy.

John: That's too bad. _____ Mexico City _____?
4   5

Emma: Well, it's huge! It's very busy and the traffic is sometimes awful.

John: Uh-huh. _____ the food?
6

Emma: It was delicious. We had fresh vegetables and fruit every day.

John: That's great!

traffic in Mexico City

the Acropolis in Athens

B. Look at the sentences you wrote in Grammar Activity C on page 142.
Discuss your trip with a partner. Use open questions to find out
more information.

A: *I traveled to Seoul last year.*

B: *What was it like?*

A: *It was fantastic. Seoul is a beautiful city. I visited …*

Unit Assignment	Give a presentation about a special city

 In this assignment, you choose a special city and give a presentation
about it. Think about the Unit Question, "What makes a city special?"
and use the Self-Assessment checklist on page 146.

CONSIDER THE IDEAS

A. What does this advertisement show about London? Check (✓) the
things on page 146. Then compare with a partner.

☐ 1.	interesting sights	☐ 8.	job opportunities
☐ 2.	good shopping	☐ 9.	friendly residents
☐ 3.	natural beauty	☐ 10.	culture
☐ 4.	great museums	☐ 11.	a variety of restaurants
☐ 5.	beautiful architecture	☐ 12.	beautiful views
☐ 6.	historic buildings	☐ 13.	clean and safe parks
☐ 7.	important monuments	☐ 14.	good public transportation

PREPARE AND SPEAK

A. GATHER IDEAS Work in a group of four. Think of a list of special cities. Why is each city special? Make notes in your notebook.

B. ORGANIZE IDEAS With your group, look at your notes from Activity A.

- Choose only one city to present to the class. Why is this city special? Write four or five reasons.
- Describe an experience you had there. What did you do? Where did you go?
- Optional: Cut out or print photos of your city. Make an advertisement like the one in Consider the Ideas.
- Each person chooses a reason to describe and gives information about an experience there.
- Practice your presentation.

 for Success

Remember: Give extra information to make your presentation more interesting.

C. SPEAK Take turns presenting information about your city. Look at the Self-Assessment checklist below before you begin.

CHECK AND REFLECT

A. CHECK Think about the Unit Assignment. Complete the Self-Assessment checklist.

		SELF-ASSESSMENT
Yes	No	
☐	☐	My information was clear.
☐	☐	I used vocabulary from this unit.
☐	☐	I used the past tense correctly.
☐	☐	I pronounced past tense verbs with -ed correctly.
☐	☐	I asked open questions during our discussions.

B. REFLECT Discuss these questions with a partner.

1. What is something new you learned in this unit?

2. Think about the Unit Question, "What makes a city special?" Do you have a different opinion now? If yes, how is your opinion different?

Track Your Success

Circle the words you learned in this unit.

Nouns
architect
architecture
climate 🔑
correction
culture 🔑 AWL
location AWL
monument
opportunity 🔑
performance 🔑
resident AWL
sight 🔑

skyscraper
variety 🔑
view 🔑

Adjectives
average 🔑
correct 🔑
historic
located AWL
recent 🔑
special 🔑
various 🔑

Verbs
correct 🔑
create 🔑 AWL
improve 🔑
locate AWL
perform 🔑
specialize

Adverbs
correctly 🔑
recently 🔑
specially

🔑 Oxford 2000 keywords
AWL Academic Word List

Check (✓) the skills you learned. If you need more work on a skill, refer to the page(s) in parentheses.

LISTENING ●	I can listen for frequency. (p. 134)
VOCABULARY ●	I can use the dictionary to identify word families. (p. 138)
GRAMMAR ●	I can use the past of *be* and simple past affirmative statements. (p. 140)
PRONUNCIATION ●	I can pronounce *-ed* endings. (p. 143)
SPEAKING ●	I can use open questions. (p. 144)
LEARNING OUTCOME ●	I can give a presentation about a special city using the simple present and simple past. (p. 145)

Interview a classmate about important events in his or her life and present them to the class.

Unit QUESTION

What are the most important events in someone's life?

PREVIEW THE UNIT

A Complete the sentences that are true for you. Add one idea. Then talk with a partner. Which events do you think were important?

1. I started doing my favorite hobby when I was _____ years old.

2. I started studying English when I was _____ years old.

3. I got my first cell phone when I was _____ years old.

4. I traveled to _____ when I was _____ years old.

5. _____

B Look at the photo. Who are the people? What are they doing?

C Discuss the Unit Question above with your classmates.

🔊 Listen to *The Q Classroom*, **Track 34 on CD 2**, to hear other answers.

149

LISTENING 1 | Ania Filochowska: A Young Genius

VOCABULARY

Here are some words from Listening 1. Read the sentences. Which explanation is correct? Circle *a* or *b*.

genius

1. Sam is a mathematical **genius**. He's very young, but he can do difficult math problems.
   a. Sam thinks math is very difficult.
   b. Sam is extremely intelligent.

2. Rob ran very fast and **won** an important race. Tom ran a little slower.
   a. Rob was first in the race.
   b. Tom was the best runner.

3. John got 100% of the answers correct on his exam. He studied a lot. He's happy about his **achievement**.
   a. John's got a good score because the exam was easy.
   b. John tried hard and did something successfully.

competition

4. Anna was in a spelling **competition** yesterday. She was nervous, but she did very well.
   a. In a competition, people try to win.
   b. In a competition, people just want to have fun.

5. At the end of the soccer game, the score was 4 to 1. Matt's team got a **prize** of $100. The other team didn't get anything.
   a. Matt's team got $100 because they won.
   b. Matt's team got $100 because they need to buy new soccer shoes.

6. Carlos **grew up** in Caracas. He left when he was 18. Now he lives in Chicago.
   a. Carlos spent his childhood in Caracas.
   b. Carlos has a lot of family in Caracas.

7. Emma studied hard and got good test scores in high school, so she **got into** a good university.
   a. Emma picked the university because the classes are hard.
   b. The university picked Emma because she's a good student.

8. Kate's exams are **over**. Now she's going to take a vacation.
   a. Kate's exams were difficult.
   b. Kate's exams are finished

PREVIEW LISTENING 1

Ania Filochowska: A Young Genius

You are going to listen to a radio quiz about a young musician, Ania Filochowska (pronounced *AN-ya fee-la-HOV-ska*). Discuss the questions.

1. Do you know other young people with very special skills or talents? Are they "geniuses"?

2. How do very young people develop or learn special skills?

COMPREHENSION CHECK

CD 2
Track 35

A. Listen to the radio quiz. Check (✓) the correct year or age for each milestone. (You will not check all the columns.)

Tip for Success

A *milestone* is an important event in someone's life.

Milestones	1993	1997	2005	6 years old	8 years old
1. Ania was born.	☐	☐	☐	☐	☐
2. She was in her first important competition.	☐	☐	☐	☐	☐
3. She began to study the violin.	☐	☐	☐	☐	☐
4. She got into a music school.	☐	☐	☐	☐	☐
5. She moved to a new country.	☐	☐	☐	☐	☐

B. Listen again. Circle the best answer to complete the sentences.

1. Ania Filochowska was born in ___.
   a. New York   c. New Jersey
   b. Poland   d. Japan

2. Ania won ___ in her first music competition.
   a. first prize   c. third prize
   b. second prize   d. money

3. Ania has ___.
   a. older brothers   c. older sisters
   b. younger brothers d. younger sisters

4. Ania ___ at the same time.
   a. studied English and went to music school
   b. went to high school and studied English
   c. studied Spanish and went to music school
   d. went to high school and music school

5. Kate (the woman on the radio) ___.
   a. won a CD of Ania's music   c. doesn't have any of Ania's CDs
   b. won tickets to Ania's concert   d. has all of Ania's CDs

WHAT DO YOU THINK?

A. Do you agree with these statements? Write A (agree) or D (disagree).

___ 1. Ania worked too hard when she was a child.

___ 2. Geniuses are different from other people.

___ 3. Everyone should play a musical instrument.

___ 4. Everyone is born with special talents.

___ 5. Schools should help all students find their talents.

___ 6. Parents should help their children find their talents.

B. Discuss your answers with a partner. Give reasons for your opinions.

Two or more events happen in a **sequence**. First one thing happens. Then another thing happens. These words and expressions can help you listen for sequence.

**CD 2
Track 36**

Sam was born **in 1992**. His family lived in Egypt, but they moved a lot.
First, they moved to Chile.
Then they lived in Singapore.
When Sam was 12, his family went to Bangkok.
Finally, they moved to Seoul. They live there now.

**CD 2
Track 37**

A. Listen to the conversation. Number the events in the correct order (1–6).

____ a. Her family moved to Boston, Massachusetts.

____ b. She got a job in a store in San Francisco, California.

_1_ c. John's grandmother was born in Jamestown, New York.

____ d. Her family lived in Philadelphia, Pennsylvania.

____ e. Her family moved to Miami, Florida.

____ f. She moved to Los Angeles, California.

**CD 2
Track 38**

B. Listen to parts of the conversation again. Circle the expressions you hear.

1. first   in 1950   then

2. in 1955   first   when I was a teenager

3. when I was ten   in 1960   then

4. when I was 18   then   in 1968

5. in 1972   finally   when I was 22

6. finally   then   in 1980

LISTENING 2 | Naguib Mahfouz: A Successful Writer

VOCABULARY

A. Here are some words from Listening 2. Read the definitions. Then complete each sentence.

> **attend** (*verb*) to go to a place, especially a school
>
> **government** (*noun*) the group of people who rule a country
>
> **graduate** (*verb*) to finish your studies at school (usually high school or college)
>
> **literature** (*noun*) books, plays, and poetry
>
> **novel** (*noun*) a book about people and things that are not real
>
> **politics** (*noun*) work and ideas connected with government
>
> **promotion** (*noun*) a more important job
>
> **retire** (*verb*) to stop working because you are a certain age

James is a manager now.

Khalid's students read a lot of books.

1. James got a(n) _____ at work. He was a salesperson. Now he's a manager.

2. Khalid teaches _____ in a university. His students read a lot of books.

3. Sam enjoys working for the Canadian _____. He meets a lot of world leaders.

4. David wants to _____ from his company next March when he turns 65 years old.

5. Mika and Emma _____ the same university. They take a lot of classes together.

6. My favorite _____ is *A Tale of Two Cities* by Charles Dickens. I read it every year.

7. There are always a lot of stories about _____ in the news. Today there was a story about the new president of Mexico.

8. Sarah plans to _____ from college this year. She should start looking for a job.

B. Answer these questions. Then ask and answer the questions with a partner.

1. What high school did (or do) you attend? _____

_____

2. When did you (or will you) graduate from high school? _____

3. Do you enjoying reading literature? _____

4. What is your favorite novel? _____

_____

5. How can you get a promotion at work? _____

_____

PREVIEW LISTENING 2

Naguib Mahfouz: A Successful Writer

You are going to listen to a presentation about Naguib Mahfouz (pronounced *na-HEEB ma-FOOS*). To prepare for the presentation, discuss the following questions.

Naguib Mahfouz

1. Who is your favorite writer? Why is this writer your favorite?

2. What are the Nobel Prizes?

COMPREHENSION CHECK

CD 2
Track 39
A. Read the sentences. Then listen. Write *T* (true) or *F* (false) for each sentence. Then correct each false statement to make it true.

_____ 1. Naguib Mahfouz grew up in Cairo.

_____ 2. He came from a large family.

_____ 3. His mother took him to movies.

_____ 4. His father was a government employee.

_____ 5. He worked for the Egyptian government.

_____ 6. He had three children.

_____ 7. He wrote only a few novels.

_____ 8. He wrote for 70 years.

CD 2
Track 39
B. Read the questions. Then listen again. Circle the correct answers.

Tip for Success

Listen carefully for numbers, like years. That will give you important information about Naguib Mahfouz.

1. What novel by Naguib Mahfouz does Hassan mention?
   a. *Party Talk*   c. *Parents' Park*
   b. *Palace Walk*   d. *Plant Talk*

2. What two subjects was Naguib Mahfouz interested in as a child?
   a. history and literature   c. history and politics
   b. literature and politics   d. mathematics and history

3. In what year did he graduate from college?
   a. 1904   b. 1913   c. 1923   d. 1934

4. How old was he when he got married?
   a. 23   b. 32   c. 34   d. 43

5. How many novels did he write?
   a. 23   b. 32   c. 34   d. 43

6. Which Nobel Prize did he win?
   a. History   b. Peace   c. Literature   d. Politics

7. How old was he when he died?
   a. 64   b. 74   c. 84   d. 94

Q WHAT DO YOU THINK?

A. What were some milestones in your life? Check (✓) them below. Add one more idea. Then compare with a partner.

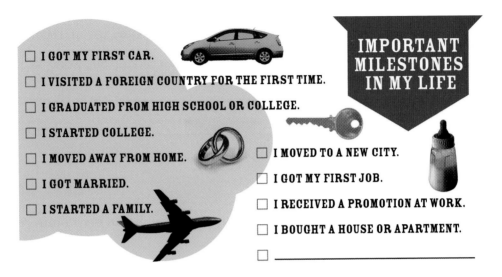

IMPORTANT MILESTONES IN MY LIFE

☐ I GOT MY FIRST CAR.

☐ I VISITED A FOREIGN COUNTRY FOR THE FIRST TIME.

☐ I GRADUATED FROM HIGH SCHOOL OR COLLEGE.

☐ I STARTED COLLEGE.

☐ I MOVED AWAY FROM HOME.

☐ I GOT MARRIED.

☐ I STARTED A FAMILY.

☐ I MOVED TO A NEW CITY.

☐ I GOT MY FIRST JOB.

☐ I RECEIVED A PROMOTION AT WORK.

☐ I BOUGHT A HOUSE OR APARTMENT.

☐ _____

Tip Critical Thinking

In Activity B, you **choose** your two most important milestones. Choosing means you have to make decisions. You use your own experiences and knowledge to make choices. This is an important thinking skill.

B. Think about both Listening 1 and Listening 2 and discuss the questions.

1. What was your first important milestone?

2. What was your most recent milestone?

3. What were the two most important milestones in your life? Why were they important?

Building Vocabulary | **Phrases with *get***

There are many phrases with the word *get*. In these phrases, *get* often means *receive* or *become*. The past tense form of *get* is *got*.

> John **got married** in 2009.
> Anna **got a job** at a big company.

More phrases with *get*		
get along	get hurt/injured	get a promotion
get better/worse	get in touch	get lost
get engaged	get in trouble	get sick
get hired	get laid off (lose a job)	

A. Complete the sentences. Use a phrase with *get* in the simple past.

Toshi and Mika

1. Mika and Toshi _____ in 2001. Now they have two children.

2. Emma graduated from college two months ago, and she wanted a job. She _____ last month. She works in a lawyer's office.

3. Carlos _____ last week. He has a terrible cold.

4. Sun-Hee _____ at work because she was late yesterday. Her boss said, "Don't be late again!"

5. Sam and Anna _____ last night. Sam took Anna to a nice restaurant and asked her to marry him.

6. James _____ because his company had a lot of problems. He is now looking for a new job.

7. Kate _____ with an old friend yesterday. She found her on a social network.

8. Emma _____ at work. She broke her leg.

9. Rob and Sam _____ well when they were young. But they aren't friends now.

10. We _____ on our way to the museum. We don't know this city very well.

B. Complete the sentences about yourself, a friend, or a family member. Then compare with a partner.

1. _____ got engaged _____.

2. _____ got married _____.

3. _____ got laid off _____.

4. _____ got hired _____.

5. _____ got a promotion _____.

6. _____ got injured _____.

SPEAKING

The simple past describes completed actions in the past.

> I **graduated** from college two years ago.
> I **started** playing the piano when I was eight years old.

Many verbs have irregular past forms. They don't end in *-ed*. For a list, see page 182.

Irregular past forms							
begin	**began**	eat	**ate**	have	**had**	read	**read**
buy	**bought**	get	**got**	make	**made**	see	**saw**
come	**came**	go	**went**	meet	**met**	take	**took**
do	**did**	grow	**grew**	put	**put**	think	**thought**

Affirmative statements		
subject	verb	
I - You - We - They	**moved**	to Chile last year.
He - She - It	**came**	at noon yesterday.

- For affirmative statements, use the same past form for all subjects.

Negative statements			
subject	*did* + not	verb	
I - You - We - They	**did not**	**move**	to Chile.
He - She - It	**didn't**	**come**	yesterday.

- For negative statements, use *did not* + the base verb for both regular and irregular verbs.

Yes/No questions				Short answers	
did	subject	verb		*yes*	*no*
Did	you	**get**	a new job?	Yes, I **did**.	No, I **didn't**.
	he	**like**	the novel?	Yes, he **did**.	No, he **didn't**.

Information questions					Answers
wh- word	*did*	subject	verb		past verb
Where		you	**go**	to school?	I **went** to school in Tokyo.
When	**did**	he	**start**	his new job?	He **started** last Saturday.
What		they	**buy?**		They **bought** a new car.

A. Complete each sentence. Use the correct simple past form. Some sentences are negative.

1. James _____ (not / go) to Beijing last year.

2. Emma _____ (eat) a delicious meal at the new Italian restaurant.

3. Kate and Matt _____ (have) a baby in November.

4. Isabel _____ (buy) a new car yesterday.

5. Carlos _____ (not / get) laid off from his job.

6. Toshi _____ (not / graduate) from college in June.

7. Mika _____ (take) a cooking class.

8. Anna _____ (retire) from teaching two years ago.

9. Sun-Hee _____ (not / give) Anna a book yesterday.

10. Rob _____ (become) a registered nurse three years ago.

Isabel has a new car.

B. Look at the underlined information in the answers below. What question does the information answer—*when, what, where,* or *why*? Write a question for each answer.

1. Question:_____

   Answer: Rob called me <u>yesterday.</u>

2. Question:_____

   Answer: He got a promotion <u>because he works really hard</u>.

Rob called me yesterday.

3. Question:_____

Answer: He went <u>to Shanghai</u> for vacation.

4. Question:_____

Answer: He bought his son <u>a bicycle</u> for his birthday.

C. What did you do yesterday? What <u>didn't</u> you do? Write sentences. Use the verbs in the box. Then read your sentences to a partner.

buy	come	do	eat	give	go
have	play	read	see	study	watch

Things I did

1. _____

2. _____

3. _____.

Things I didn't do

4. _____

5. _____

6. _____

Numbers ending in -*teen* (*13* and *14*) and numbers ending in -*ty* (*30* and *40*) can be difficult to pronounce. These numbers sound similar, but you pronounce the second syllable differently.

CD 2
Track 40

Numbers with -*teen* The second syllable starts with a hard "t" sound and ends with "n."	Numbers with -*ty* The second syllable uses a soft "d" sound, like "dee".
13 "thir-teen"	30 "thir-dee"
14 "four-teen"	40 "four-dee"
15 "fif-teen"	50 "fif-dee"

A. Listen to the sentences. Circle the number that you hear. Then practice the sentences with a partner.

1. My cousin is (13 / 30) years old.

2. She was born in (1916 / 1960).

3. The shirt cost (15 / 50) dollars.

4. She graduated at the age of (18 / 80).

5. The president died in (1913 / 1930).

6. He retired (13 / 30) years ago.

7. They went to Oman (14 / 40) years ago.

8. The plane ticket was (414 / 440) dollars.

9. His great-grandfather was born in (1914 / 1940).

10. The train left at (4:15 / 4:50).

The train left at . . .

B. For each item, write a sentence with one of the numbers. Then read your sentences to a partner. Listen to your partner's sentences. What number do you hear?

 for Success

If you don't
understand a
number, you can
ask a question
like, "Did you say
thirteen—one-three?"

1. (13 / 30) _____

2. (14 / 40) _____

3. (15 / 50) _____

4. (16 / 60) _____

5. (17 / 70) _____

In this assignment, you interview a classmate about important events in his or her life. Then you give a presentation about them. As you prepare, think about the Unit Question, "What are the most important events in someone's life?" and use the Self-Assessment checklist on page 164.

CONSIDER THE IDEAS

A. Read the sentences about the milestones in Toshi's life. Match each milestone with the correct detail.

Toshi

Milestones	Details
1. Toshi's family moved to Tokyo. ____	a. He got stronger and faster, and and he made a lot of friends.
2. He joined a soccer team in middle school. ____	b. He studied computer engineering, and he learned a lot.
3. His grandfather died. ____	c. He was Toshi's best friend. He always had time to talk to Toshi.
4. He started taking chess lessons. ____	d. Tokyo had good middle schools. His old city didn't have good schools.
5. He started college in Osaka. ____	e. He made new friends from different countries, and his English improved a lot.
6. He came to London to study English. ____	f. He really enjoyed learning something new. He still plays a lot, and he enters competitions.

Skill Review | **Using open questions**

Remember: Ask open questions to get answers with more information. Review the Speaking Skill box in Unit 9, page 144.

A: In 2006, I went to India.
B: What was it like?

A: I came to this school last year.
B: Why did you choose this school?

PREPARE AND SPEAK

A. **GATHER IDEAS** Interview your partner. Follow these steps.

1. Start with a general question like, "What were the important events in your life?"

2. Ask follow-up questions for details and reasons, for example, "When did that happen?" and "Why was that important?"

3. Get information about at least six milestones. Write your partner's milestones and details in your notebook.

   Anna visited Brazil. This was important because Anna's father is from Brazil. Anna met her grandparents and her aunts and uncles. She is very close with them now.

B. **ORGANIZE IDEAS** Choose four of your partner's milestones to present to your class.

   • Write your presentation in your notebook.
   • Include at least two details about each milestone.

C. **SPEAK** Tell your class about your partner's milestones. Look at the Self-Assessment checklist below before you begin.

CHECK AND REFLECT

A. **CHECK** Think about the Unit Assignment. Complete the Self-Assessment checklist.

		SELF-ASSESSMENT
Yes	No	
☐	☐	My information was clear.
☐	☐	I used vocabulary from this unit.
☐	☐	I used the past tense correctly.
☐	☐	I used expressions with *get* correctly.
☐	☐	I pronounced numbers correctly.

B. **REFLECT** Discuss these questions with a partner.

1. What is something new you learned in this unit?

2. Think about the Unit Question, "What are the most important events in someone's life?" Do you have a different answer now than when you started the unit? If yes, how is your answer different?

Track Your Success

Circle the words you learned in this unit.

Nouns	Adjective	Phrases
achievement 🔑 AWL	over	get along
competition 🔑	**Verbs**	get better/worse
genius	attend	get engaged
government 🔑	get into	get hired
literature 🔑	graduate	get hurt/injured
novel 🔑	grow up	get in touch
politics 🔑	retire	get in trouble
prize 🔑	win 🔑	get a job
promotion AWL		get laid off
		get lost
		get married
		get a promotion
		get sick

🔑 Oxford 2000 keywords

AWL Academic Word List

Check (✓) the skills you learned. If you need more work on a skill, refer to the page(s) in parentheses.

LISTENING	⬤	I can identify a sequence. (p. 153)
VOCABULARY	⬤	I can understand many phrases with *get*. (p. 157)
GRAMMAR	⬤	I can use the simple past with regular and irregular verbs. (p. 159)
PRONUNCIATION	⬤	I can pronounce numbers with *-teen* and *-ty* . (p. 161)
SPEAKING	⬤	I can use open questions. (p. 163)
LEARNING OUTCOME	⬤	I can interview a classmate about important events in his or her life and present them to the class. (p. 163)

Audio Scripts

Unit 1: People

The Q Classroom Page 3

Teacher: Today we are beginning Unit One. Every unit in Q starts with a question. We will talk about this question again while we study the unit. The question for Unit One is: "What are you interested in?" How about you, Yuna? What are you interested in?

Yuna: I like movies.

Teacher: OK. Yuna likes movies. How about you, Felix? What are you interested in?

Felix: I'm interested in music. I play the guitar. I want to learn more instruments.

Teacher: Oh, very good. Marcus, what are you interested in?

Marcus: Lots of things. I really like sports.

Teacher: What's your favorite sport?

Marcus: Soccer. I play soccer every weekend.

Teacher: So Felix plays guitar and Marcus plays soccer. How about you, Sophy? What are you interested in?

Sophy: I like art. I like to go see art, and I also like to paint and draw.

Teacher: So, you all have different hobbies and interests. We'll talk about them more as we complete Unit One.

LISTENING: Are You Interested in Art?
Comprehension Check Page 6

Part 1

Lin: Excuse me. Can I sit here?

James: Sure. Hi. My name is James. What's your name?

Lin: Hi, James. I'm Lin.

James: It's nice to meet you, Lin. I like your hiking boots.

Lin: Thanks. I go hiking a lot.

James: Really?

Lin: Yes, I go hiking with my friends every weekend. Do you ever go hiking?

James: Uh, no, not really. I usually watch a movie on the weekend. Or I go to a museum. Uh, are you **interested in** art?

Lin: Yes, I am. And I really like movies, too.

James: Oh, great! Well, you know, there's a movie **club** here.

Lin: Really? Do you **belong to** the movie club at this school?

James: Yes, I do. It's a lot of fun. We see a movie every Thursday.

Part 2

David: Hi, Anna. Is that a good book?

Anna: Oh, hi, David. Yes, it's great! It's for my book club.

David: Oh. Do you read a lot of books in your book club?

Anna: Well, we usually read one book every month. So that's 12 books a year.

David: That's a lot.

Anna: Do you belong to a book club, David?

David: No, I don't, but I have some **hobbies**. I **collect** comic books and I play soccer. Uh, do you play soccer?

Anna: Yes, I play with my brother. He's **good at** soccer. He goes to this school, too. He's on the soccer team.

David: Really? I'm on the soccer **team**, too.

Anna: Maybe you know my brother! His name is Rob.

David: Let me think. Is he tall with short brown hair?

Anna: Yes, that's him!

Part 3

Mika: Hi. Is this Professor Kim's music history class?

Sam: Yes, it is. Are you a new student?

Mika: Yes, my name is Mika.

Sam: Hi, Mika. I'm Sam. Uh, where are you from?

Mika: I'm from Japan.

Sam: Oh. Uh, is this your first music class?

Mika: No, it's not. I play the guitar. How about you? Do you play an **instrument**?

Sam: No, I don't play an instrument, but my father plays the piano. I like sports. I play soccer and tennis. Are you interested in sports?

Mika: Yes, I am. Tennis is my favorite sport!

BUILDING VOCABULARY: Collocations for hobbies and interests
A. Page 7

Speaker: Liz Alan lives **in** Toronto. She works at the after-school program at the community center in her town. Children come to the community center after school. Liz does many activities with them. It's a good job for her because she is interested **in** a lot of different things. She is good **at** sports. She also likes music and she can **play** the guitar. She sings songs with the kids. The kids can also **take** piano and guitar lessons. On sunny days, Liz and the kids **ride** bikes or **go** hiking. Sometimes they go **to** the beach or the park. On rainy days, Liz and the kids **watch** DVDs, or they **play** games like chess and checkers. Sometimes they go to a museum together. After work, Liz sometimes gets **together** with friends, but she usually goes home to relax and **read** a book.

B. Page 8

1. **Sun-Hee:** I'm Sun-Hee. I'm a teacher. I really like my job, but I'm very busy. On the weekends, I relax and read books. I'm also interested in sports. My favorite sport is swimming. I go to the beach every Saturday.

2. **Khalid:** My name is Khalid. I'm from Oman and I'm a computer programmer. I play a lot of video games. I also ride my bike on the weekends.

PRONUNCIATION: Simple Present third-person -s/-es
Page 12

gets

makes

listens

plays

watches

washes

A. Page 12

1. He goes shopping on Saturdays.
2. Khalid works downtown.
3. Sam plays video games in the evening.
4. Sun-Hee sometimes watches TV after work.
5. Mary gets together with friends on Sundays.
6. Mika lives in Los Angeles.
7. David washes his car on Saturdays.
8. Emma belongs to a golf club.

SPEAKING SKILL: Keeping a conversation going, Part 1
Page 13

A: Rome is my favorite city. What's yours?

B: Bangkok.

A: Rome is my favorite city. What's yours?

B: Bangkok. It has amazing buildings and delicious food!

A: I like cooking. How about you?

B: I like cooking, too.

A: I like cooking. How about you?

B: I like cooking, too. I often cook with friends on the weekends.

SPEAKING SKILL: Keeping a conversation going, Part 2
Page 14

Hmm.

Let's see.

Let me see.

Let me think.

Uh.

Well.

A. Page 14

Tom: Carlos, what's your favorite sport?

Carlos: Uh, it's soccer. But I also like basketball. What's yours?

Tom: Hmm. It's probably volleyball. I play on the beach in the summer.

Carlos: Where's your favorite beach?

Tom: Let me see. Miami has a really good beach.

Carlos: Well, what's your favorite beach near *here*?

Tom: Ocean Beach is my favorite. It's beautiful. Do you know any beaches near here?

Carlos: Let me think. Well, I like East Beach. It has really big waves. People surf there.

UNIT ASSIGNMENT: Consider the Ideas
B. Page 15

Good afternoon. This is my friend Ivan. Ivan is from Russia. He's a computer engineer. Ivan is interested in hiking in the mountains. He goes hiking once a month. Ivan is good at soccer. He belongs to a soccer club and plays every weekend. Ivan also plays the piano. He gets together with his friends to play classical music. Ivan sees a lot of movies. His favorite movie is *Avatar*.

Unit 2: Friendship

The Q Classroom   Page 19

Teacher: The Unit Two question is: "How do you make friends?" What do you think, Marcus? How do you make friends?

Marcus: I'm on a soccer team, so I make a lot of friends there. I have friends on my team and on the other teams.

Teacher: OK, so that's one way to make friends. You can join a team. What do you think, Sophy? How do you make friends?

Sophy: I study at the tables by the cafeteria. A lot of students go there to study, and I meet some nice people.

Teacher: Hmm, so that's a good place to make friends, but maybe it's not a great place to study! So Marcus plays soccer and Sophy studies by the cafeteria. What about you Felix?

Felix: I make friends in my classes and at work. I like to talk, so I meet people in many places.

Teacher: Good point. Some activities help you make friends, but your personality can also help you make friends. Yuna, how do you make friends?

Yuna: I'm in the chemistry club and the cooking club.

Teacher: Clubs are a great way to meet people with your interests. We'll talk more about making friends as we go through Unit Two.

LISTENING: Making Friends
Comprehension Check   Page 22
Part 1

Rob: Welcome to *Talk of the City*. I'm Rob Stevens and we're talking about making friends. My first guest is Katie Jones, a teacher at Greendale College. Welcome, Katie.

Katie: Thank you.

Rob: Uh, Katie, is it hard for some students to make friends?

Katie: Oh, yes. It's a very big problem for some college students.

Rob: What **advice** do you give your students?

Katie: Well, I usually say, "Don't stay at home. Go out and talk to people."

Rob: Uh-huh. What else?

Katie: I also say, "**Join** a club or a team." It's important to **share** interests with other people. For example, I love hiking. I belong to a hiking club.

Rob: Thank you, Katie. That's all good advice.

Part 2

Rob: My next guest is David Scott. Hi, David.

David: Hi, Rob.

Rob: David, you're a **volunteer**. Is that a good way to make friends?

David: Oh, yes. Volunteers are very **positive**. Positive people make friends easily.

Rob: What do you do as a volunteer?

David: I go to the beach every Saturday morning with a group of people. We pick up garbage on the beach.

Rob: Are you friends with the other volunteers?

David: Oh, yes, I am. Three of the volunteers are my **close** friends. We do a lot of fun things together. We usually have breakfast before we go to the beach on Saturdays.

Rob: Sounds fun. Thanks, David.

Part 3

Rob: Our last guest today is Dr. Mary Johnson, a counselor for young people. It's nice to meet you, Dr. Johnson.

Dr. Johnson: Nice to meet you, too, Rob.

Rob: Dr. Johnson, how can people make friends?

Dr. Johnson: Well, first, everybody knows, "Friendly people make a lot of friends." So, when you meet new people, **smile** and look at them. Just be friendly.

Rob: Mm-hmm. But some people are very shy. What can shy people do?

Dr. Johnson: Well, shy people usually don't talk very much, but a shy person can give people compliments. For example, say, "That's a nice tie."

Rob: That's true.

Dr. Johnson: Yes. Or a shy person can ask people questions, like "What do you do on the weekend?" And then just listen.

Rob: That's great advice. Thank you. Now we can take some questions.

BUILDING VOCABULARY: Word categories

B. Page 23

1. **John:** Bye, Yoshi. I have to go.

   Yoshi: Where are you going, John?

   John: I'm going to chorus.

   Yoshi: Chorus? What's that?

   John: Uh, it's a singing group.

   Yoshi: A singing group? That sounds like fun.

   John: Yes, it's a great hobby.

   Yoshi: What kind of music do you sing?

   John: We sing a lot of folk music.

   Yoshi: Folk?

   John: Yes, it's a kind of traditional music.

   Yoshi: Oh, yes! I love traditional music.

2. **Emma:** Amanda, you're so good at math. This class is really hard for me.

   Amanda: Is this your first calculus class, Emma?

   Emma: Yes, it is. How about you?

   Amanda: No, this is my second calculus class. You can look at my notes.

   Emma: Oh, thanks! Can I look at them now?

   Amanda: Well, right now I'm going to lacrosse practice.

   Emma: What's lacrosse?

   Amanda: It's a type of sport. We practice on the big field behind the library.

   Emma: Oh, right.

   Amanda: But I can meet you at the library after practice.

   Emma: Really? Thanks.

3. **Matt:** What are you reading about, David?

   David: Oh, hi, Matt. I'm reading about the history of the blues.

   Matt: The blues? What's that?

   David: It's a type of music. It's from the southern part of America.

   Matt: Oh, that sounds interesting.

   David: What about you, Matt? What are you reading?

   Matt: I'm reading an article about rugby. It's a kind of sport. It's sort of like American football.

   David: Yeah, I know that game. My brother plays rugby.

4. **Mary:** Excuse me. I really like your shoes.

   Sarah: Oh, thank you.

   Mary: Are they for running?

   Sarah: No, they're for racquetball.

   Mary: What's racquetball?

   Sarah: It's a type of sport. It's like tennis.

   Mary: Oh, I see.

   Sarah: I think I know you. Are you in my physics class?

   Mary: Do you mean Professor Lee's physics class?

   Sarah: Yes, that's it.

   Mary: Yes, I am! My name is Mary.

   Sarah: Hi, Mary. My name is Sarah. It's nice to meet you.

LISTENING SKILL: Listening for examples

Page 24

I meet new people in a lot of different places, like the library or the coffee shop.

Matt is always busy. For example, he takes Spanish lessons on Thursdays, he plays tennis on Saturdays, and he works five days a week.

A. Page 24

Kate: Hi, Sun-Hee! How are you? Do you like your new school?

Sun-Hee: Hi, Kate! I'm so happy to see you! Um, I like my school, but I miss my friends here at home. I don't have any friends at school.

Kate: Oh, I'm sorry to hear that.

Sun-Hee: You make friends really easily, Kate. Do you have any advice?

Kate: Well. Let me see. Do you belong to any clubs, like the computer club or the movie club?

Sun-Hee: Well, I belong to the chess club, but I don't really like it.

Kate: OK. What are you interested in?

Sun-Hee: Well, I'm very interested in languages. For example, I love French and Spanish!

Kate: Then join the French club and talk to some new people.

Sun-Hee: But I'm a little shy. What do I say?

Kate: It's easy. Talk about topics like movies and classes. You can ask people questions. For example, you can ask "What's your favorite movie?" or "What classes do you have?"

Sun-Hee: That's a good idea.

Kate: Do you talk to people in your classes?

Sun-Hee: Yes, there are some nice girls in my biology class.

Kate: Great. Ask them to go out after class, like to a coffee shop or the library.

Sun-Hee: That's good advice. Thanks, Kate.

B. Page 24

1. **Sun-Hee:** You make friends really easily, Kate. Do you have any advice?

   Kate: Well. Let me see. Do you belong to any clubs, like the computer club or the movie club?

2. **Kate:** OK. What are you interested in?

   Sun-Hee: Well, I'm very interested in languages. For example, I love French and Spanish!

3. **Kate:** Then join the French club and talk to some new people.

   Sun-Hee: But I'm a little shy. What do I say?

   Kate: It's easy. Talk about topics like movies and classes.

4. **Kate:** Do you talk to people in your classes?

   Sun-Hee: Yes, there are some nice girls in my biology class.

   Kate: Great. Ask them to go out after class, like to a coffee shop or the library.

PRONUNCIATION: Sentence intonation
Page 27

I have a problem. (falling intonation)

He doesn't play sports. (falling intonation)

Do you belong to a club? (rising intonation)

Does she live in China? (rising intonation)

What do you mean? (falling intonation)

When does it start? (falling intonation)

A. Page 28

1. Does your brother play baseball? (rising intonation)
2. What classes do you have today? (falling intonation)
3. Do you have any advice? (rising intonation)
4. I don't know David. (falling intonation)
5. I'm in the book club. (falling intonation)
6. Do you like soccer? (rising intonation)
7. How about you? (falling intonation)
8. Sometimes I play basketball. (falling intonation)
9. Where does the tennis club meet? (falling intonation)
10. He doesn't make friends easily. (falling intonation)

UNIT ASSIGNMENT: Consider the Ideas
Page 28

Female 1: Good afternoon. We are presenting four good ways to make friends here in Portland. First, become a volunteer. For example, I work at the food bank downtown. We give food to hungry families. I work with wonderful people, and they are now my friends. My brother reads to children at the library on Saturdays. He makes new friends every week.

Male 1: Second, join a club. In our city, we have a lot of clubs. For example, we have a movie club and a Spanish club. Some clubs are very small, like the chess club. The chess club has only ten members. In a small club, you make friends fast.

Female 2: Third, join a team, like the soccer team or swimming team. I'm on the lacrosse team. Every Sunday, we play against teams from all over the city.

Male 2: Finally, take a class, like an art class or a cooking class. I take a cooking class. The class meets on Saturday mornings. We make delicious food. It doesn't cost a lot, and I meet new people. Those are our ideas. Thank you! Do you have any questions?

Unit 3: Education

The Q Classroom Page 33

Teacher: Today we're going to talk about the Unit Three question: "What makes a good school?" What do you think, Felix?

Felix: For me, a good school is a small school. In a small school, the students and the teachers all know each other.

Teacher: Felix likes a small school. Do you agree, Sophy?

Sophy: Not really. I like large schools because they have more clubs, more subjects, and more teachers. So you can choose the things you want.

Teacher: How about you, Marcus? What do you think makes a good school?

Marcus: Well, I'm interested in sports, so good sports teams are important to me.

Teacher: What do you think, Yuna? What makes a good school?

Yuna: Technology is important. A good school should have new technology, like computers in the classrooms.

Teacher: These are some good points. We'll talk more about schools as we study Unit Three.

LISTENING: Let's Take a Tour
Comprehension Check Page 36

Sarah: Good afternoon, everyone. Welcome to your **campus** tour. I'm your tour guide, Sarah Carter. I'm a student here at Watson University. We have a beautiful campus. Follow me so I can show you the school. . . . This is our library. It has a lot of books and new computers. And it has free **Internet access**. Students can bring their own computers here and go online. Behind the library, there is a sports field for many of our teams, like the lacrosse and soccer teams. Now look to the left. This is the dining commons. Students eat meals here. Next to the dining commons is one of the dormitories.

Female 1: Excuse me. How many dormitories are there?

Sarah: There are four large dormitories. All of our students live here on campus. Do you have any other questions?

Male 1: Yes, I do. Are the classes here big or small?

Sarah: Well, there are only about 2,000 students here, so the classes are small. I think that's very important. We talk to our **professors** every day, and they know us well. In small classes, teachers have time to make **special** lessons for their students. That way, the lessons are interesting for everyone. Also, the classes here are very **active**. We don't just sit and listen to the teacher. For example, we work in teams and we have discussion groups in class.

Also, here at Watson University, students learn important **skills**, like writing skills and critical thinking. We study **foreign languages**, too, and we learn about the world. Many students study in other countries for a semester. For example, my friend Carlos is studying history in France right now. Yes?

Female 1: I have a question. The school is in a small town. Do students go into town a lot?

Sarah: Yes, they do. Watson is a wonderful small town. Students go into town for many reasons. They can relax and go to dinner or a movie there. They can also help the **community**. For example, many students become volunteers. They help at places like the food bank and the hospital. OK. Let's continue our tour.

PRONUNCIATION: Sentence stress
Page 41

There are <u>two</u> <u>sports</u> <u>fields</u>.

The <u>museum</u> is <u>not</u> <u>interesting</u>.

We go to <u>school</u> in a really <u>dangerous</u> <u>neighborhood</u>.

Do you <u>have</u> a <u>class</u> <u>today</u>?

A. Page 41

1. Does the <u>school</u> have a <u>lacrosse</u> <u>team</u>?
2. I have <u>two</u> <u>classes</u> in the <u>morning</u>.
3. We <u>want</u> a <u>safe</u> and <u>clean</u> <u>school</u>.
4. The <u>college</u> is in a <u>dangerous</u> <u>city</u>.
5. The <u>coffee</u> <u>shops</u> have <u>free</u> <u>Internet</u> <u>access</u>.
6. <u>What</u> is a <u>good</u> <u>school</u>?
7. Our <u>sports</u> <u>field</u> is pretty <u>big</u>.
8. My <u>school</u> is <u>really</u> <u>great</u>!
9. The <u>buses</u> to his <u>school</u> are <u>very</u> <u>slow</u>.
10. <u>When</u> does the <u>class</u> <u>begin</u>?

SPEAKING SKILL: Giving opinions
Page 42

A: I think that students need computers.

B: In my opinion, small classes are important.

A: I think that our school is great.

B: I agree. I think that the classes are interesting.

C: I disagree. In my opinion, the classes are too big.

A. Page 42

1. **A:** In my opinion, a good school gives a lot of tests. Then students study every day.

   B: I disagree. Class discussions make students study.

2. **A:** I think that sports are really important. Students need healthy bodies.

   B: I agree. Exercise is very important.

3. **A:** In my opinion, the food in our dining commons isn't very good. I don't like it!

   B: I agree. I think that it tastes terrible. I usually cook my own food.

4. **A:** In my opinion, we need a new library. The building is really old.

   B: I disagree. I like our library. I think that it's beautiful.

5. **A:** Our school isn't in a good neighborhood. I think that it's very dangerous. I hear police sirens all the time.

   B: I disagree. You hear sirens because the police station is on the same street! In my opinion, the school is very safe.

UNIT ASSIGNMENT: Consider the Ideas
Page 43

Amanda: Good afternoon. Today we are presenting our plan for the perfect school. First, in our opinion, a perfect school is large. Big schools have many sports teams and classes. The school is big, but the classes are very small. There are about ten or fifteen students in a class. In small classes, students can talk to the professor and do interesting activities.

Rob: Our perfect school has a big gym with a swimming pool. We like to exercise. Also, the students at our school get free computers, and they can have free Internet access in the school.

Kate: Our perfect school is in a small town. Small towns are really safe and the people are friendly. In the town, students can go to restaurants, movies, parks, and coffee shops. They can also live in the town. Apartments are large and beautiful, and they are not very expensive.

James: There are two very special things about our school. First, students don't pay for food on campus. All the food is free. Second, on the last day of school every year, there is a concert on campus. That's the end of our presentation. Thank you. Do you have any questions?

Unit 4: Food

The Q Classroom Page 47

Teacher: The Unit Four question is: "How do you choose your food?" Let's start with Yuna. What is important to you when you choose your food, Yuna?

Yuna: I like healthy food. Not too much fat.

Teacher: Good for you! How about you, Felix? Do you eat healthy food?

Felix: Not always. I'm busy, and sometimes I just eat something because it's fast and easy, like pizza from the cafeteria.

Teacher: Hmm, so you often choose food because it's convenient. Sophy, how do you choose your food?

Sophy: Fresh food is very important to me. I eat a lot of vegetables, and I don't like food with lots of sugar or salt.

Teacher: So Yuna avoids eating fat and Sophy avoids eating sugar and salt. How about you, Marcus? How do you choose your food?

Marcus: Well, I don't eat very much meat. But I eat most other things. I love spicy food and sweets.

Teacher: You have mentioned nutrition, convenience, and taste. These are all good reasons for choosing food. We'll look more at these reasons as we go through Unit Four.

LISTENING: Lifestyles and Food Choices
Comprehension Check Page 50

Part 1

Kate: Hi, what's your name?

Carlos: Carlos.

Kate: Carlos, how do you choose your food?

Carlos: Well, I'm an athlete, so I'm very careful about food.

Kate: Uh-huh. How are you careful?

Carlos: Well, for example, I'm a **vegetarian**.

Kate: A vegetarian. Uh-huh.

Carlos: Yes, and I try to eat only **organic** fruits and vegetables.

Kate: Do you *ever* eat meat?

Carlos: No, I don't. In my opinion, meat is bad for your heart.

Kate: Mm-hmm. Well, thank you, Carlos.

Part 2

Kate: Hi, what's your name?

Mika: I'm Mika.

Kate: Hi, Mika. Tell me: How do you choose your food?

Mika: Well, I really enjoy cooking. I love to try new foods and taste new **flavors**.

Kate: Do you cook for other people?

Mika: Oh, yes, I like cooking for my friends. I invite friends over for dinner every Saturday night.

Kate: That sounds like a lot of fun. So, are you a very **social** person?

Mika: Oh, yes. And I think meals are a social time. My friends and I eat and talk and have a great time together.

Kate: Great. Thanks, Mika.

Part 3

Kate: Hi. What's your name?

Matt: My name is Matt.

Kate: OK, Matt. . . . How do you choose your food?

Matt: Hmm. Well, I try to choose healthy food. . . . I **avoid** food with a lot of fat or salt. For example, I buy nonfat milk.

Kate: I see. And what do you like to eat?

Matt: Uh, well, I eat a lot of fresh fruits and vegetables. And I eat a lot of fish.

Kate: Why do you like those foods?

Matt: Because they're really **nutritious**, in my opinion. . . . You see, I'm 71 years old, and my doctor is worried about my health. I try to listen to my doctor's advice.

Kate: Great. Thanks for talking to me, Matt.

Part 4

Kate: Hi, what's your name?

Sarah: Hi, I'm Sarah.

Kate: Hello, Sarah. I see you're buying some frozen dinners.

Sarah: Yeah, I know they have a lot of **artificial** ingredients, but I can't cook at home. I don't have a kitchen. I'm a student, and I live in a dormitory.

Kate: I see. Do you ever eat in the dining commons on your campus?

Sarah: Sometimes, but I'm really busy. I have five classes and I work three days a week. I eat a lot of frozen food and fast food because it's cheap and **convenient**.

Kate: You're right about that! Thanks for talking to me, Sarah.

PRONUNCIATION: Stressed syllables
Page 52

organic

vegetarian

unfriendly

A. Page 52

1. delicious [del<u>i</u>cious]
2. allergic [all<u>er</u>gic]
3. unhealthy [unh<u>eal</u>thy]
4. education [educ<u>a</u>tion]
5. convenient [conv<u>e</u>nient]
6. sugar-free [sugar-<u>free</u>]
7. garden [<u>gar</u>den]
8. dinner [<u>din</u>ner]

9. non<u>dai</u>ry
10. com<u>mu</u>nity

B. Page 53

1. In my <u>opinion</u>, <u>artificial</u> <u>ingredients</u> are <u>unsafe</u>.
2. He <u>doesn't</u> eat <u>chicken</u> or <u>beef</u>.
3. He <u>wants</u> to <u>lose</u> <u>weight</u>, so he's on a <u>diet</u>.
4. This <u>soup</u> has an <u>unusual</u> <u>flavor</u>.
5. Are these <u>cookies</u> <u>sugar-free</u>?
6. She <u>grows</u> <u>organic</u> <u>tomatoes</u> in her <u>garden</u>.

C. Page 53

Listen again to Activity B.

LISTENING SKILL: Listening for reasons
Page 53

A: Why do you eat sugar-free food?

B: Because sugar is bad for your teeth.

A: Why don't you eat fast food?

B: Because it has artificial ingredients in it.

A. Page 53

1. **Friend:** These apples look good, John. Do you want to get some?

   John: Um, are they organic?

   Friend: Uh, no, they're not.

   John: Well, I only buy organic apples.

   Friend: Really? Why?

   John: Because in my opinion, they have a great flavor. They taste delicious.

2. **Amanda:** Would you like a snack?

   Friend: Sure, thanks, Amanda. Do you have anything sweet, like some cookies or ice cream?

   Amanda: Oh, sorry, I don't buy fattening foods, like cookies and ice cream.

   Friend: Really? Why not?

   Amanda: Because I want to lose ten pounds.

3. **Friend:** James? Do you want to come to my house tonight and make dinner?

   James: Uh, no, let's go out for dinner.

   Friend: But, James, I have a lot of food at home. Why do you want to go out?

   James: Because I'm a terrible cook. I burn everything.

4. **Friend:** Hey, Anna. Let's go out and get some food. I'm really hungry.

   Anna: OK. Let's go to Kay's Kitchen. It's my favorite restaurant.

   Friend: Really? Why is it your favorite restaurant?

   Anna: Because it's near my house. It's on the corner of my street! I eat there almost every night!

GRAMMAR: Verbs + gerunds or infinitives
A. Page 56

1. I don't like to cook.
2. You need to eat more vegetables.
3. I enjoy shopping for food.

4. I avoid buying food with artificial ingredients.

5. I try to eat only organic food.

6. She wants to avoid meat.

7. He can't stand cooking.

8. We love eating fast food.

9. In my country, we like to eat a lot of rice.

10. He hates going to the supermarket.

UNIT ASSIGNMENT: Consider the Ideas
Page 57

Female student: Hi, can I interview you about your food choices?

Male student: Uh, sure.

Female student: OK. What's your favorite food?

Male student: Well, I think pizza's my favorite food.

Female student: And why is it your favorite?

Male student: Because it's cheap and convenient. Also, I love cheese.

Female student: OK. Um, do you think organic food is good for you?

Male student: I really don't know. I don't buy it.

Female student: Why not?

Male student: Because in my opinion, it's too expensive.

Female student: OK. And what kinds of food do you avoid?

Male student: Let's see. I try to avoid strawberries.

Female student: Why do you avoid strawberries?

Male student: Because I'm allergic to them.

Female student: OK. And what do you usually eat for breakfast?

Male student: Nonfat yogurt.

Female student: Why do you choose nonfat yogurt?

Male student: Well, it fills me up and gives me energy.

Female student: OK. Great. That's it. Thanks a lot!

Unit 5: Fun

The Q Classroom Page 61

Teacher: Today we're going to talk about the Unit Five question: "What makes something fun?" How about you, Sophy? What do you like to do for fun?

Sophy: I like to go to galleries and museums. I like to look at art.

Teacher: Why is that fun?

Sophy: It's interesting for me because I like to paint and draw.

Teacher: How about you, Yuna? What makes something fun?

Yuna: Being with lots of people.

Teacher: OK, so you like social activities. How about you, Marcus? What do you think makes something fun?

Marcus: Being active. Playing a sport, or hiking or biking. Physical activities are the most fun for me.

Teacher: How about you, Felix? What makes something fun?

Felix: I agree with everyone. I like art shows and being with lots of people and being active. But I also like relaxing, like reading in the park or lying on the beach. That's fun, too.

Teacher: Yes, there are a lot of different ways to have fun. We'll talk more about these things as we study Unit Five.

LISTENING: Why Do You Come to the Park?
Comprehension Check Page 64

Mary: Today, I'm in Ibirapuera Park in São Paulo, Brazil. It's a very large park, and it has something for everyone. For example, there are hiking **paths**, sports fields, and beautiful gardens. But there are also museums and other important buildings. Let's speak with some people in the park. Hi there. What's your name?

Isabel: I'm Isabel.

Mary: Hi, Isabel. Why do you come to this park?

Isabel: I come here because it's so much fun!

Mary: What exactly makes it fun?

Isabel: Well, for me it's fun because I learn a lot here. For example, I love learning about art. I go to the Museum of **Modern** Art every week. And I like to look at the beautiful sculptures all around the park.

Mary: Yes, there is a lot of art in the park. Why else do you come to the park?

Isabel: Hmm. My friends and I come here because we love music. There are **concerts** in the park. They're great because they're free and they're **outdoors**!

Mary: Thanks, Isabel.

Mary: Let's talk to someone else. Hello, sir, what's your name?

Carlos: Hi, I'm Carlos.

Mary: Hi, Carlos. How do you like the park?

Carlos: I really like it a lot. I always have a lot of fun here.

Mary: Why is it fun for you?

Carlos: Well, let me think. I like to be active. There is a lot to do here. I play soccer with my friends. Sometimes my friends and I ride our bikes around the park. We also like to go hiking on the paths.

Mary: That sounds like fun. What's another reason?

Carlos: Uh, well, because I love to be in **nature**. I like to look at the trees and gardens. It's beautiful here and very **relaxing**. It's very **crowded** in the city. But it's nice and quiet in the park.

Mary: Yes, it is beautiful. Thanks, Carlos. . . . So it sounds like Ibirapuera Park is a great place for everyone. You can come here for art, music, sports, or just to have fun with friends.

PRONUNCIATION: Reduced pronouns
Page 70

I think he's at the park

I don't see him.

Is that her bike?

Let's call them.

He's at the park.

A. Page 71

1. **A:** John is a fun guy. How do you know him? Does he play soccer with you?

   B: No. I know him from school. How do you know him?

   A: He spends time at the park near my house. Sometimes he plays basketball there with my friends and me.

2. **A:** Anna's sister Emma is here this weekend. Do you know her?

   B: Yes, I do. I really like her.

   A: Me too. Do you think Anna and Emma want to see a movie with us tonight?

   B: Maybe. Let's call them.

SPEAKING SKILL: Agreeing and disagreeing
Page 72

A: I like swimming.

B: I do too.

A: I like swimming.

B: Me too.

A: I don't like swimming.

B: I don't either.

A: I don't like swimming.

B: Me neither.

A: I think that the sculpture is pretty.

B: Oh, I don't know.

A: I love that park. How about you?

B: I'm not sure.

A. Page 72

1. **Anna:** This is a great concert. I love this band.

   Sun-Hee Me too. Let's buy their CD!

2. **Anna:** I love this park. It's my favorite park in the city. How about you?

   Sun-Hee Uh, I'm not sure. It's really crowded.

3. **Anna:** I never go skiing. I think it's too dangerous. What about you?

   Sun-Hee Oh, I don't know. I think skiing is fun.

4. **Anna:** I don't like this movie.

   Sun-Hee I don't either. I think it's terrible.

5. **Anna:** I think this class is really fun.

   Sun-Hee I do too. I'm learning a lot!

6. **Anna:** I don't like to play video games.

   Sun-Hee: Me neither. I think they're boring.

UNIT ASSIGNMENT: Consider the Ideas
A. Page 73

Female 1: OK. What are your favorite places?

Male 1: Uh, I really like going to the city park because there are a lot of fun things to do there.

Female 2: Me too. I like to go hiking and play tennis there.

Male 2: Well, I really like the movie theater. I love seeing movies.

Female 2: I do too. I go to the movies a lot.

Female 1: And how about the Modern Art Museum?

Male 1: Um, I don't know. I don't really like going to the museum. Why do you think it's fun?

Female 1: I think that it's fun because you learn a lot about art.

Male 1: OK. I see. So, what's another good place?

Female 1: I really like the shopping mall.

Male 2: Me too. I like to go there with my friends. Sometimes I meet them there after work.

Female 1: Why do you like it?

Male 2: Because there's great food and sometimes there's live music.

Female 2: Well, I don't know. I like to go shopping, but I don't really like the mall.

Male 1: I don't either. But how about the beach? I love the beach.

Male 2: Me too. It's a really fun, social place.

Female 1: And how about downtown? I like to go shopping there.

Female 2: I do too. And there are a lot of great restaurants. What do you think?

Male 1: I'm not sure. Everything is really expensive downtown.

Unit 6: Home

The Q Classroom Page 77

Teacher: The Unit Six question is: "What makes a good home?" How about you, Yuna? Are you happy with your home now?

Yuna: Yes, I am.

Teacher: What do you like about it?

Yuna: My roommates are nice.

Teacher: Yes, the people you live with are very important. How about you Felix? What do you think makes a good home?

Felix: Location is important. I like my home because I can walk to school and to the store—it's really convenient.

Teacher: Marcus, what do you think? What makes a good home?

Marcus: Right now I think a good home is quiet. My neighbors are really noisy. Sometimes I want to move, but my apartment is cheap.

Teacher: What do you think makes a good home, Sophy?

Sophy: Hmm, I want three bathrooms, a big backyard, and a swimming pool. And I want to be right next to the beach!

Teacher: (Laughs) Well, I hope you can live in that home someday! There are many different reasons to choose a home. We'll talk more about this as we go through Unit Six.

LISTENING 1: How Do You Like Your Home?
Comprehension Check Pages 79–80
Part 1

Amanda: Hi, everyone.

All: Hi, Amanda. / Hello. / How are you?

Amanda: I'm OK. Listen: I need some advice. I want to move because my apartment is too far from school, but I don't know where to live. John, you live in a dormitory on campus, right?

John: Yes, I do.

Amanda: Do you like it?

John: Well, no, I don't like it very much.

Amanda: Why not?

John: Because I don't have a **private** room. I share a room with a **roommate**. I like him, but our room is really small. And it's really **noisy**. I want to live alone.

Amanda: Mm-hmm. So, do you like anything about the dorm?

John: Yes. I generally like the people in my dormitory. We talk and have a lot of fun together.

Amanda: Well, that sounds good.

John: And the **location** is great. It's really near my classes.

Part 2

Amanda: Mary, where do you live?

Mary: I live in a studio on First Street.

Amanda: How is it?

Mary: It's great! I'm a very private person, so I really like living alone.

Amanda: It's a studio. Is it really small?

Mary: Yes, it's pretty small, but it's very **comfortable**.

Amanda: What do you think of the location?

Mary: The location is really good. There are a lot of coffee shops and stores near my building. Also, I can walk to class in 15 minutes.

Amanda: Are there any problems?

Mary: Well, my **rent** is pretty expensive.

Amanda: Oh. The location sounds nice, but I can't pay a lot of rent.

Part 3

Amanda: Carlos, where do you live now?

Carlos: I live at home with my extended family. I live with my parents, my two brothers, my grandmother, and my aunt.

Amanda: So how do you like it?

Carlos: I like it because I like my family. Also, I don't pay rent.

Amanda: But it sounds like a lot of people. Is it very crowded?

Carlos: Not really. There are six bedrooms and three bathrooms. But it's pretty noisy sometimes. It's difficult to study.

Amanda: How about the location?

Carlos: Well, the house is far from campus, so I take a bus. But it's near **public transportation**.

Amanda: Well, my family doesn't live around here, so I can't live with them.

LISTENING SKILL: Listening for opinions
Page 81

I think that this house is very beautiful.

I think the location is very good.

I love this apartment.

It's expensive.

The rent is only $400 a month.

Page 82

1. **Sam:** What do you think, Rob?

   Rob: Well, Sam, I think the location is excellent.

   Sam: Uh-huh. It's across the street from our school. We can walk to class!

   Rob: Yes, and the rent is only $800 a month.

   Sam: I think it's perfect.

2. **Mary:** Mom, I want to move.

   Mother: Why? What's wrong with your apartment, Mary?

   Mary: Well, it's far from the school campus, and I hate taking the bus.

   Mother: Mm-hmm. What else is wrong?

   Mary: I have bad neighbors. They stay up late and play loud music.

3. **Matt:** Hi, James.

   James: Matt, it's good to see you. Come in.

   Matt: Wow, your new house is beautiful.

   James: Thanks. I'm really happy with it.

   Matt: How many bedrooms does it have?

   James: It has only two bedrooms.

   Matt: Oh.

4. **Mika:** How do you like your new apartment, Kate?

   Kate: Well, the living room is pretty small and dark.

   Mika: That's too bad.

   Kate: Yeah, but the kitchen is big and sunny.

   Mika: Oh, that's great. You love to cook. Where is it?

   Kate: It's on Baker Street. It's near your house, Mika.

   Mika: That's great. And it's only five minutes from the school.

LISTENING 2: Housing Problems, Housing Solutions
Comprehension Check Pages 84–85

Good evening. I'm Dr. Ross Chan and I'm talking today about **housing**. We have a beautiful new university in Jackson, but the campus is small and we don't have enough dormitories for all of our students. We have a housing **shortage**. There is some housing in town, but many apartments aren't **affordable** for students, so they don't have many choices.

Some students live in small, inexpensive apartments downtown. These apartments are near public transportation, restaurants, and stores. There is also a lot of **entertainment** downtown on Market Street. But the downtown area is dangerous at night, and the apartments are in old buildings. The buildings are in bad **condition**. And even these apartments are starting to become expensive. **Landlords** are **increasing** rents because there is a **demand** for these apartments.

So what is another choice for students? Well, some other students share houses near campus with friends. These houses are in safe neighborhoods, but they are expensive and they are very crowded and noisy. Students can't study at home, and sometimes they can't get enough sleep.

Other students live at home with their families. They live in a safe space, and they don't pay rent. But this choice is not possible for all students. Many of them move here from different cities, and their families live far away.

We at the university are all very worried about this problem. We have a wonderful new university. It can increase business in Jackson. But new students need housing. The city wants the university to grow, so we need to build safe, affordable apartments and houses for our students.

PRONUNCIATION: Stress in compound nouns
Page 87

post office

bookshelf

drugstore

A. Page 87

1. **a.** swimming <u>pool</u>

   b. <u>swimming</u> pool

2. a. <u>boo</u>kshelf

  b. book<u>shelf</u>

3. a. <u>bed</u>room

  b. bed<u>room</u>

4. a. shopping <u>mall</u>

  b. <u>shopping</u> mall

5. a. drive<u>way</u>

  b. <u>drive</u>way

6. a. <u>post</u> office

  b. post <u>office</u>

7. a. grand<u>son</u>

  b. <u>grand</u>son

8. a. mail<u>box</u>

  b. <u>mail</u>box

9. a. <u>living</u> room

  b. living <u>room</u>

10. a. <u>fire</u>place

  b. fire<u>place</u>

UNIT ASSIGNMENT: Consider the Ideas
Page 91

Student 1: Good afternoon. This is our presentation about a good home. Inside the house, there are four bedrooms and three bathrooms. There is a really big living room with comfortable chairs and sofas. There are big windows in all the rooms.

Student 2: Outside the house, we have a big backyard. There is a table with chairs. We have a lot of trees and flowers. We also have a swimming pool. It's very relaxing in our backyard.

Student 3: We have a very nice neighborhood. The house is in a good location. It is across the street from a beautiful park with a lot of trees. It's near public transportation and the supermarket. We also have very nice neighbors. Thank you for listening. Do you have any questions?

Unit 7: Weather

The Q Classroom Page 95

Teacher: In Unit Seven, we'll be discussing the question: "How does the weather affect you?" How about you, Marcus? What's your favorite kind of weather?

Marcus: I like warm, sunny weather.

Teacher: Why?

Marcus: Because I like to be outdoors and be active. I hate being stuck inside because of the weather.

Teacher: What about you, Yuna? Do you like warm, sunny weather?

Yuna: Yes, of course.

Teacher: How does it make you feel?

Yuna: Warm weather makes me happy. I feel sad when it's raining.

Teacher: So Marcus and Yuna both like warm weather. How about you, Felix? How does the weather affect you?

Felix: I don't mind cold weather; I'm happy to wear a sweater or a coat, but I don't like the rain. When it rains, I just want to sleep.

Teacher: How does the weather affect you, Sophy?

Sophy: I don't think the weather affects me very much. I like hot days and cold days, and sometimes I like the rain, too. But, of course, I don't like to be freezing or really hot. The weather only affects me when it's really bad.

Teacher: OK, we'll talk more about weather and our feelings as we study Unit Seven.

LISTENING 1: The World of Weather
Comprehension Check Pages 97–98

John: Welcome to the *World of Weather*. I'm John Radley.

Mary: And I'm Mary Beckford. Let's look at the weather around the world right now. We have some unusual weather today, John.

John: Yes, we do. We have very cold **temperatures** in Asia today. It's minus two degrees in Tokyo, Japan and minus ten degrees in Beijing, China right now. Snowstorms are **affecting** travel all over Asia. They're **causing delays** in most airports, and the airports in Tokyo and Beijing are closed.

Mary: That's right, John. And another **effect** of the snow and ice is broken **power** lines. Thousands of people in parts of Asia don't have power right now.

John: Now let's look at the Middle East. It's extremely hot in parts of the Middle East today. Cairo, Egypt has a temperature of 43 degrees. And it's 45 degrees in Jeddah, Saudi Arabia. It's also very windy. The wind is causing **severe** sand storms. So try to stay inside today.

Mary: Turning to Europe: Most major European cities have nice weather today. It's 12 degrees in Paris, France, right now. In London, England, it's 14 degrees. You need a jacket, but it's beautiful and sunny outside.

John: In most parts of South America today, it's very warm. The temperature in Rio de Janeiro, Brazil, is currently 27 degrees. Unfortunately, there is a lot of rain in Rio today, and the rain is causing **floods**.

Mary: But on the other side of South America, the weather is beautiful and dry. The temperature in Lima, Peru, today is 22 degrees.

John: Finally, let's look at the United States. The weather on the East Coast of the U.S. is very cold today. There is a lot of snow here in New York, and we have a temperature of minus three degrees. In most parts of the West Coast, it's nice and warm. Los Angeles, California, has a temperature of 22 degrees today. People are out and having fun.

Mary: Oh, I think 22 degrees sounds very nice, John.

John: I agree, Mary. It sounds wonderful. . . . And that's our weather for this hour. Come back at 2 p.m. for our next weather report.

LISTENING 2: Weather and Our Moods
Comprehension Check Page 100

Good evening. I'm Dr. Sarah Jones and I'm here to talk about some ways that the weather can affect our **moods**.

To start, let's think about the effects of nice weather. Some people like to take vacations at the beach. Why? Because the beach is usually sunny and warm. When people go on vacation, they want to relax and feel good. Warm, sunny weather often makes people feel **cheerful**. Sunlight affects our brains. It makes us happy. When the weather is sunny and beautiful, people want to be active and go outside. They get together with friends, swim, play games, and go hiking.

Now, let's think about the effects of bad weather. In northern countries, some people have a problem called seasonal affective disorder—or S-A-D, SAD—**during** the winter. This problem usually occurs in places with cold, dark winters. What causes SAD? Doctors aren't sure, but they think sunlight is a big factor. People need sunlight. In many places, the sunlight **decreases** during the winter. When people don't get enough sunlight, they sometimes develop SAD.

SAD has several **symptoms**. First, SAD makes people feel sad or **depressed**. They also feel tired, and they don't want to do anything. They sleep a lot. People with SAD sometimes eat a lot, so they gain weight. Many people become very quiet, and they don't talk to their family or friends very much.

Interestingly, very hot weather can have similar effects. Some places in the world have extremely hot temperatures in the summer. When it's very hot, people often don't go outside. They stay inside, close the windows, and shut the curtains. Because of this, sometimes they don't get enough sunlight. They feel tired and they eat a lot—just like people with SAD do. There are other effects of extremely hot weather, too. For example, it sometimes makes people feel **irritable** and angry.

It's clear: The weather can affect our moods. So the next time you want to change your mood, just wait for the weather to change. Thank you. Are there any questions?

SPEAKING SKILL: Asking for repetition
Page 105

A: It's hot today!

B: Excuse me?

A: It's very hot today.

B: Yes, it is.

A: The weather report is on.

B: Sorry. What did you say?

A: I want to listen to the weather report.

B: Oh, OK.

A: What's the temperature today?

B: It's 13 degrees.

A: I'm sorry. Could you repeat that?

B: Sure. It's 13 degrees.

A. Page 106

1. **A:** It's really cold in Seoul today.
   B: Excuse me?
   A: Seoul is cold today.
   B: Oh, really?

2. **A:** What's the temperature right now?
   B: It's 30 degrees.
   A: I'm sorry. Could you repeat that?
   B: The temperature is 30 degrees.

3. **A:** I'm flying to London today.
   B: But the airport is closed! There's a big snowstorm in London.
   A: Sorry. What did you say?
   B: The airport is closed today. It's snowing very hard.
   A: Oh, no!

4. **A:** I love this hot, sunny weather.
   B: Excuse me?
   A: I love this beautiful weather.
   B: Oh, me too!

PRONUNCIATION: Stressing important words
Page 107

A: Excuse me. Where does this bus go?

B: It goes <u>downtown</u>.

A: It's 13 degrees in Mexico City today.

B: Excuse me? <u>30</u> degrees?

A: No, <u>13</u> degrees.

A. Page 107

1. **A:** Is the airport closed?
   B: No, it's <u>open</u>.

2. **A:** What's the weather like in Madrid?
   B: It's very <u>cold</u>.

3. **A:** What kind of weather do you like?
   B: Well, I really like <u>hot</u>, <u>sunny</u> weather.

4. **A:** Do you want to go shopping?
   B: No, I don't want to go <u>shopping</u>. I want to go <u>swimming</u>.

5. **A:** It is 14 degrees in Dubai today?
   B: No, it's <u>40</u> degrees.

UNIT ASSIGNMENT: Consider the Ideas
Page 109

Student 1: OK. We're discussing the question, "How does the weather affect you?"

Student 2: Well, winter has a really good effect on me. I love winter sports, like skiing and snowboarding.

Student 3: Oh, not me. I hate winter. I have a long drive to work. When it snows, I have to stay home. Also, I don't like being cold. I have an electric heater for my room, but it's expensive. The winter weather has a bad effect on my life.

Student 4: I agree with you. I always catch a cold. I get sick every winter.

Student 1: Well, I just don't think that weather affects my life.

Student 2: Sorry. What did you say?

Student 1: Uh, I don't think that weather affects me at all. I always get to work. I don't get sick. I don't love or hate any kind of weather.

Student 2: Uh, that's pretty interesting. It's a really different opinion.

Student 3: I don't know. I think weather affects all of us.

Student 1: I'm not so sure about that. . . .

Unit 8: Health

The Q Classroom   Page 113

Teacher: The Unit Eight question is: "What do you do to stay healthy?" So let's talk about our healthy habits. How about you, Yuna?

Yuna: I eat healthy food and I exercise every day.

Teacher: Good for you! How about you, Marcus? Do you eat healthy food and exercise?

Marcus: Well, I exercise a lot, but my diet isn't that great. I eat too much sugar.

Teacher: How about you, Sophy?

Sophy: I get some exercise. I go swimming once or twice a week, and I eat a lot of vegetables. But I don't sleep enough. I think I get sick too often because I don't sleep enough.

Teacher: Felix, what do you do to stay healthy?

Felix: Well, I don't have Sophy's problem! I get eight hours of sleep every night, and I always make time to relax. My diet isn't that good though. I need to cook more. I eat out too much.

Teacher: You all sound pretty healthy! We'll talk about more ways to stay healthy as we go through Unit Eight.

LISTENING 1: Health Watch
Comprehension Check   Pages 115–116

Sylvia: Hi. Welcome to *Health Watch*, show number 42. This is the weekly podcast to teach you about health. I'm your host, Sylvia Wong. I'm here today with Dr. Michael Smith. He's here to talk to us about **stress**. Dr. Smith, why is stress a big problem these days?

Dr. Smith: Well, Sylvia, it's a very big problem for several reasons. First, everyone is very busy. For example, a lot of people work full time and have children. They don't have time to relax.

Sylvia: That's true. *I'm* very busy. What's another reason?

Dr. Smith: Another cause of stress is money. Money problems are often very stressful.

Sylvia: How about students? Do they have a lot of stress?

Dr. Smith: Oh, many students have serious problems with stress. Sometimes they take classes and they work, so they're very busy. They also feel stress because they worry about their grades.

Sylvia: Right. Grades can be very stressful.

Dr. Smith: Yes, and new students sometimes feel **lonely** because they don't have friends. This can also cause stress.

Sylvia: I see. And what are the symptoms of stress?

Dr. Smith: Well, stress can make people feel really tired. They don't have any energy. They become **run-down** and they get sick often. Stress can even make people gain weight.

Sylvia: So, Dr. Smith, we all have *some* stress. How can we **manage** our stress?

Dr. Smith: Well, there are several ways to **reduce** stress. First, you should exercise. After work, you should go for a walk in a park or around the neighborhood. **Diet** is also extremely important. People should eat a lot of fruit and vegetables.

Sylvia: Okay, so exercise and diet are important. What are some other ways to reduce stress?

Dr. Smith: Well, people should have social time with friends. Laughter is a great way to reduce stress.

Sylvia: You're right! I always feel better after a fun day with my friends. Well, Dr. Smith, thank you for the excellent advice!

Dr. Smith: You're welcome.

LISTENING SKILL: Listening for Frequency
Page 117

A: Do you **always** exercise at the gym?

B: No, **sometimes** I jog in the park.

A: How often do you exercise?

B: **Three times a week.**

A. Page 117

1. **Anna:** John, how are you doing?

   John: Hi, Anna. I'm not doing very well. I'm always tired these days. I can't sleep.

2. **Anna:** John, that's terrible! What's going on?

   John: Well, I have a lot of stress at work. I work every day. I don't get a day off.

3. **Anna:** That's too much! How often do you exercise?

   John: I never exercise. I just don't have time.

4. **John:** How about you? How often do you exercise?

   Anna: Me? I exercise six days a week.

5. **John:** Really? That's wonderful! Do you go to a gym?

   Anna: Sometimes. I exercise at a gym three times a week. But I also like to go running and play tennis.

6. **John:** How often do you go running?

   Anna: I go running twice a week. It's fun. I usually go to the park near my house.

7. **Anna:** So, are you eating well?

   John: Not really. I usually eat fast food for lunch. And I always drink coffee with my meals.

8. **Anna:** Oh, John! You should make some changes in your life. Just do one thing differently. For example, maybe you can try to exercise three times a week.

   John: That's good advice. Thanks, Anna!

B. Page 118

Anna: John, how are you doing?

John: Hi, Anna. I'm not doing very well. I'm always tired these days. I can't sleep.

Anna: John, that's terrible! What's going on?

John: Well, I have a lot of stress at work. I work every day. I don't get a day off.

Anna: That's too much! How often do you exercise?

John: I never exercise. I just don't have time. How about you? How often do you exercise?

Anna: Me? I exercise six days a week.

John: Really? That's wonderful! Do you go to a gym?

Anna: Sometimes. I exercise at a gym three times a week. But I also like to go running and play tennis.

John: How often do you go running?

Anna: I go running twice a week. It's fun. I usually go to the park near my house. So, are you eating well?

John: Not really. I usually eat fast food for lunch. And I always drink coffee with my meals.

Anna: Oh, John! You should make some changes in your life. Just do one thing differently. For example, maybe you can try to exercise three times a week.

John: That's good advice. Thanks, Anna!

LISTENING 2: How Often Do You Work Out?
Comprehension Check Page 120

Part 1

Maria: I'm Maria Sanchez, and I'm here at a new gym. Sam's Gym is one week old today. I'm talking to some of the gym's members about their health **habits**. . . . This is Matt. Hi, Matt. How often do you work out?

Matt: Well, Maria, I work out seven days a week from 6 a.m. to 8 a.m. I really like to **stay in shape**!

Maria: Wow, you get up early!

Matt: Yes, well, I go to work at 9 a.m. I can't exercise in the evenings. I'm a manager at a busy clothing store. I usually work until 10 p.m.

Maria: Ten p.m.? How many hours do you usually sleep a night?

Matt: Well, I sleep about five hours a night. When I get home from work, I **prepare** my lunch and my dinner for the next day.

Maria: What do you make?

Matt: I usually make a salad for lunch. For dinner, I usually make chicken and vegetables.

Maria: That sounds like a healthy diet. Well, thanks for talking to me.

Part 2

Maria: Now let's talk to Kate. Kate, do you work out **regularly**?

Kate: Yes, I work out **at least** three times a week.

Maria: That's great. And do you usually eat healthy food?

Kate: Well, not really. I don't like to cook, so I eat a lot of junk food and fast food.

Maria: I see. And what do you do to stay healthy?

Kate: Well, I'm a lawyer. I work seven days a week. My job is really stressful, so I like to do relaxing activities.

Maria: What do you do to relax?

Kate: Well, for example, I like reading and walking in the park. . . . And I always get eight hours of sleep a night!

Maria: Sleep is important! Thanks a lot, Kate.

Part 3

Maria: Let's talk to Rob now. Rob, how do you stay healthy?

Rob: Well, I **watch what I eat**. I eat a lot of fresh fruits and vegetables. I'm a vegetarian. Also, I get about ten hours of sleep every night.

Maria: Ten hours. Wow. That's a lot. What do you do **for a living**, Rob?

Rob: I'm a history teacher. I love my job. I work about five hours a day.

Maria: That sounds great! And how often do you work out?

Rob: Well, actually, I never work out. This is my first time at a gym.

Maria: Really? Do you like it here?

Rob: Uh, it's a nice gym, but I hate exercising!

Maria: Well, I hope you it **keep** it **up**, Rob. Exercise is important!

PRONUNCIATION: *Can, can't, should,* and *shouldn't*
Page 124

She can swim.

She can't swim.

He can speak English.

He can't speak English.

He should sleep more.

He shouldn't eat so much.

She should exercise more.

She shouldn't work so much.

A. Page 125

1. You shouldn't eat that.
2. John should get together with his friends tonight.
3. He can play soccer very well.
4. She can't swim.
5. Kate can drive a car.
6. I should go to the gym in the mornings!
7. You shouldn't go to work today.
8. I can't go away this weekend.
9. We shouldn't go to that restaurant.
10. Carlos can't ride a bike.

UNIT ASSIGNMENT: Consider the Ideas
A. Page 126

Rob: OK, Amanda, let's go over the results of our survey.

Amanda: OK. Let's look at the first question: How many hours do you sleep every night?

Rob: Two people sleep about eight hours every night.

Amanda: I'm sorry. What did you say?

Rob: Two people sleep eight hours a night. And one person sleeps about ten hours a night.

Amanda: That's a long time! I can't sleep for ten hours.

Rob: Me neither.

Amanda: Let's look at the second question: How often do you exercise?

Rob: Let's see. One person exercises about twice a week. One person exercises four times a week. And one person never exercises.

Rob: I'm surprised. Everyone in this class looks really healthy.

Amanda: I know. I'm surprised, too.

Rob: OK. Now let's look at the third question: What do you do to relax?

Amanda: Let's see. One person walks on the beach. Two people spend time with friends.

Unit 9: Cities

The Q Classroom Page 131

Teacher: The Unit Nine question is: "What makes a city special?" How about you, Felix? What city do you want to visit and why?

Felix: I want to go to Barcelona because the buildings there are very interesting. I like to see unusual buildings.

Teacher: Yes, nice buildings can make a city very interesting. What else makes a city special? Sophy?

Sophy: Of course I'm interested in cities with a lot of art, like nice museums. Some cities also have an area with a lot of galleries. I like that a lot.

Teacher: Marcus, what do you think makes a city special?

Marcus: I like a city with good restaurants and a lot of places to go.

Teacher: So, I think that all of you like to visit big cities. How about you, Yuna? Do you think a small town can be interesting?

Yuna: Yes. My favorite place to visit is a small town in the mountains. It's next to a lake and it's very beautiful.

Teacher: That sounds nice! As we study Unit Nine, we'll talk about more things that make a city special.

LISTENING 1: Travel Talk
Comprehension Check Pages 133–134

David: Good evening, and welcome to *Travel Talk*. Tonight we're talking about three special cities. And we have three visitors to talk to us about them. Let's start with Amanda. Hi, Amanda. What city is special for you?

Amanda: Hi, David. Well, I visited Ubud last month. It's on the island of Bali in Indonesia.

David: How was it?

Amanda: It was fantastic, David! I loved the beautiful old buildings. And the food was delicious.

David: How was the weather?

Amanda: Well, Bali has a very warm **climate**. The **average** temperature is usually about 26 degrees, but in Ubud we walked through the forests, and it was very cool and comfortable.

David: Was there a lot to do?

Amanda: Oh, yes. Ubud is a center for the **culture** of Bali. I listened to live music and watched dance **performances** every night.

David: Ubud sounds like a fantastic city. Thanks, Amanda! Next, let's talk to Sam. Hi, Sam. What city do you want to talk about?

Sam: David, I **recently** visited Bruges, a city in Belgium. It's a beautiful city. The **architecture** is amazing! I enjoyed seeing **historic** buildings, like city hall. And there were art museums all over the city.

David: That sounds great. How was the food?

Sam: The food was delicious. In my opinion, Bruges has the best chocolate in the world.

David: I agree. I love Belgian chocolate! Thanks, Sam. . . . And finally, let's talk to Mika. Mika, you recently visited New York City.

Mika: Yes, I was there just last week!

David: So, how was it?

Mika: It was great. I love New York. I go there every year. Everything is big and modern and busy. There are over eight million people in New York City! There are huge skyscrapers everywhere! And the museums, like the Metropolitan Museum of Art, are big too.

David: What were your favorite things about New York?

Mika: Well, the shopping is great. I shopped every day in really big department stores and little shops all over the city. I also loved the restaurants and cafes. New York has every kind of food in the world. I tried Ethiopian food for the first time!

David: Well, thank you, everyone, for telling us about three special cities.

LISTENING 2: Making Positive Changes
Comprehension Check Pages 136–137

Mayor: Good afternoon, everyone. Welcome to Seacliff's city council meeting. Thank you for coming! Before we start the meeting, I want to talk a little bit about last year. We were all very busy. We wanted to make some important changes in our city.

Ten years ago, a lot of tourists visited Seacliff. They enjoyed our quiet city. They liked to come here for relaxing weekends. But then, we started having problems. Our city didn't have a lot of money. When the tourists stopped coming, the money problems got worse. But we have wonderful **residents** here in Seacliff, and things are getting better. We all worked very hard last year, and the city is **improving**. Let's talk about the problems and the solutions.

First of all, our parks and beaches were very dirty. There was broken glass and garbage everywhere. Last year, many of our residents volunteered to clean them up. They worked hard, and the beaches are parks are beautiful again. Everyone can enjoy them—tourists, residents, adults, and children.

Second, as you all know, we have several historic buildings and **monuments** in Seacliff. For example, in front of city hall, there is a sculpture of the city's first mayor. And next to city hall, we have the area's first hospital. It's a very beautiful building. These are very important **sights** for visitors, but they were in extremely bad condition. Hundreds of residents gave money to the city, and we used it to pay for repairs and improvements.

Third, we improved the downtown area. A few years ago, a lot of the shops closed. Business was bad and people didn't like to go downtown. But last year, a new hotel opened. The rooms have beautiful **views** of the ocean. Tourists started coming, and that **created** a lot of job **opportunities** for our residents. Many new businesses opened in that area. Now we have a **variety** of new stores and restaurants downtown, and so business is very good.

I'm very excited about all of these changes, and I want to thank everyone here. Now let's move on to new business.

PRONUNCIATION: *-ed* endings
Page 143

walked

liked

traveled

loved

visited

wanted

A. Page 143

1. They **collected** shells on the beach in Oman.

2. We **tried** to go to the Modern Art Museum.

3. He **shopped** all afternoon.

4. We **started** our tour at noon.

5. I **worked** in Dubai last year.

6. Heavy traffic **caused** problems in Los Angeles.

SPEAKING SKILL: Using open questions
Page 144

A: I visited Hong Kong last week.

B: Was it fun?

A: Yes.

A: I visited Hong Kong last week.

B: How was it?

A: It was great. I visited a lot of interesting sights, and I tried new food.

A. Page 144

Emma: John, how was Greece?

John: Fantastic! I liked Athens a lot. The museums and architecture were great. And the view from the top of the Acropolis was amazing!

Emma: What was the food like?

John: Well, Greeks eat a lot of bread, cheese, olives, and vegetables. For meat, they eat a lot of lamb. I love all of those foods, so I was very happy!

Emma: That sounds great, John.

John: How was your trip to Mexico City?

Emma: It was good, but I was really busy.

John: That's too bad. What's Mexico City like?

Emma: Well, it's huge! It's very busy and the traffic is sometimes awful.

John: Uh-huh. How was the food?

Emma: It was delicious. We had fresh vegetables and fruit every day.

John: That's great!

Unit 10: Milestones

The Q Classroom Page 149

Teacher: The Unit Ten question is: "What are the most important events in someone's life?" Yuna, what was one important event in your life?

Yuna: Starting college.

Teacher: Yes, that's a big one. You started a new school *and* you moved away from home. How about you, Marcus? What was an important event in your life?

Marcus: Getting my driver's license was important for me. It gave me a lot of freedom.

Teacher: Yuna and Marcus both mentioned common *milestones* in people's lives: going away to school and getting a license. What are other important events in someone's life?

Sophy: Getting your first job… or moving.

Teacher: Yes, those are very important. What else?

Felix: Getting my first guitar was an important event in my life. Learning how to play guitar completely changed my life.

Teacher: That's interesting. We'll talk more about important events in our lives as we study Unit Ten.

LISTENING 1: Ania Filochowska: A Young Genius
Comprehension Check Pages 151–152

Matt: Good morning, listeners. Thank you for listening to KCLM, your classical music station. I'm Matt Miller. We have some exciting news today. Ania Filochowska, is in town. This young violin **genius** is giving a concert tonight. Our next listener can play to win tickets to Ania's show. You just have to answer a few questions about Ania. The phones are ringing. Congratulations, you're my first caller! What's your name?

Kate: Hi, my name is Kate.

Matt: Hi, Kate! Are you ready to play?

Kate: I think so. I'm a big fan of Ania! I really like her.

Matt: OK, I'm going to ask you some questions about Ania's

achievements. Here's your first question: When was Ania Filochowska born?

Kate: Um, Ania was born in 1993.

Matt: That's right! Now question number 2: Where was she born?

Kate: I think she was born in Poland. Is that right?

Matt: Yes, that's correct. But what city was she born in? I'll give you a hint. It's the capital of Poland.

Kate: Oh, Warsaw!

Matt: Correct. Now, this question is a little harder. When was Ania in her first important music **competition**?

Kate: Um, I think it was when she was nine. Is that right? I know she won third **prize**.

Matt: Oh, well, you're right about the prize. She won third prize. But she was *eight* when she won the competition. Okay, on to Question 4: When did Ania begin to study violin?

Kate: Oh, I know this one! She began to study violin at the age of six.

Matt: That's correct. Ania **grew up** in a very musical family. Her older brothers play violin and viola. Now question 5: What happened to Ania in 2005?

Kate: Um, Ania **got into** the Juilliard School, the famous school for music and art in New York City. Then in September 2005, Ania moved to the United States.

Matt: Right again! You really know a lot about Ania! In the next few years, Ania studied at Juilliard and she went to high school in New Jersey, near New York City. She won many more prizes and performed in many different countries. Well, the quiz is **over**. You did a great job, Kate.

Kate: Did I win the tickets?

Matt: Yes, you did, Kate! You have two free tickets to tonight's concert!

Kate: That's great! Thank you!

Matt: You're welcome, Kate. Enjoy the show!

LISTENING SKILL: Listening for sequence
Page 153

Sam was born in 1992. His family lived in Egypt, but they moved a lot.

First, they moved to Chile.

Then they lived in Singapore.

When Sam was 12, his family went to Bangkok.

Finally, they moved to Seoul. They live there now.

A. Page 153

John: Grandma, where were you born?

Grandmother: Well, I was born in Jamestown, New York, in 1950.

John: That was a long time ago.

Grandmother: It certainly was.

John: Where did you grow up?

Grandmother: Oh, let me see. I grew up Jamestown. But we moved a couple of times. First, we moved to Philadelphia, Pennsylvania.

John: You lived in Philadelphia?

Grandmother: Yes, I did. Then we moved to Boston, Massachusetts.

John: Wow! You moved around a lot! Where did you go after that?

Grandmother: When I was 18, we moved to Miami, Florida.

John: So, when did you move to California?

Grandmother: Well, let me think. Oh, yes. I came to California when I was 22. A friend of mine worked in a store in San Francisco. She found me a job there.

John: How long did you stay in San Francisco?

Grandmother: I stayed there for about ten years.

John: And then you came here to Los Angeles?

Grandmother: Yes, finally, in 1982, I moved for the last time.

B. Page 153

1. **John:** Grandma, where were you born?

   Grandmother: Well, I was born in Jamestown, New York, in 1950.

2. **John:** Where did you grow up?

   Grandmother: Oh, let me see. I grew up Jamestown. But we moved a couple of times. First, we moved to Philadelphia, Pennsylvania.

3. **John:** You lived in Philadelphia?

   Grandmother: Yes, I did. Then we moved to Boston, Massachusetts.

4. **John:** Wow! You moved around a lot! Where did you go after that?

   Grandmother: When I was 18, we moved to Miami, Florida.

5. **John:** So, when did you move to California?

   Grandmother: Well, let me think. Oh, yes. I came to California when I was 22. A friend of mine worked in a store in San Francisco. She found me a job there.

6. **John:** How long did you stay in San Francisco?

   Grandmother: I stayed there for about ten years.

   John: And then you came here to Los Angeles?

   Grandmother: Yes, finally, I moved for the last time.

LISTENING 2: Naguib Mahfouz: A Successful Writer
Comprehension Check Page 156

Professor Jones: Good morning, everyone. I really enjoyed reading your reports. As you know, we're having student presentations today. Who wants to go first?

Hassan: I'll go first, Professor Jones.

Professor Jones: Thank you, Hassan. Please go ahead.

Hassan: OK. I wrote my report about the writer Naguib Mahfouz. He wrote the **novel**, *Palace Walk*. Mahfouz was born in Cairo, Egypt in 1911. He came from a large family. There were seven children. When he was a child, Mahfouz read a lot of books. He became very interested in history because his mother often took him to museums.

Mahfouz was also interested in **politics** because his father worked for the **government**. You can see his interest in history and politics in his novels. Mahfouz grew up and **attended** school in Cairo. He **graduated** from Cairo University in 1934. Yes, Sarah? Do you have a question?

Sarah: Excuse me, Hassan. What year did he graduate from college?

Hassan: It was 1934. Now, where was I? Oh, yes. During most of his life, Mahfouz worked in a variety of government offices. He spent many years in the Ministry of Culture. He got many **promotions** and often had important jobs in the government. At the age of 43, he got married and had two children. He finally **retired** in 1972. During his life, he wrote 34 novels and hundreds of other stories. He wrote books for 70 years. In 1988, he won the Nobel Prize for **Literature**. He lived a very long life and died at the age of 94 in 2006. Are there any questions? Yes, Toshi. Do you have a question?

Toshi: Yes. How many novels did he write?

Hassan: He wrote 34.

Toshi: Thank you.

Hassan: You're welcome. Are there any other questions? OK. Thank you for listening.

Professor Jones: Thank you very much, Hassan. That was a very interesting presentation.

PRONUNCIATION: Numbers with *-teen* and *-ty*
Page 161

Thirteen

Thirty

Fourteen

Forty

Fifteen

Fifty

A. Page 162

1. My cousin is 30 years old.
2. She was born in 1916.
3. The shirt cost $15.
4. She graduated at the age of 80.
5. The president died in 1913.
6. He retired 30 years ago.
7. They went to Oman 14 years ago.
8. The plane ticket was $440.
9. His great-grandfather was born in 1914.
10. The train left at 4:50.

Spelling of Simple Present Third-Person Verbs

Use the base verb + -s or -es after *he*, *she*, and *it*.	
Add -s after most verbs.	gets, listens, likes, plays
Add -es after -ch, -sh, or -o.	does, goes, washes, watches
If the verb ends in a consonant + -y, change the y to i and add -es.	cries, flies, studies, tries
Irregular third-person form	have → **has**

Spelling of Simple Past Verbs

Add -ed after most verbs. Add -d after verbs that end in -e.	travel**ed**, walk**ed** welcome**d**, improve**d**
If a <u>one-syllable</u> verb ends in vowel + consonant, double the consonant and add -ed.	plan**ned**, stop**ped**
If the verb ends in a consonant + -y, change the y to i and add -ed.	stud**ied**, tr**ied**
If the verb ends in vowel + -y, add -ed.	play**ed**, stay**ed**

Common Irregular Verbs

Base form verb	Past form	Base form verb	Past form
be	was, were	know	knew
become	became	leave	left
begin	began	lose	lost
break	broke	make	made
bring	brought	meet	met
build	built	pay	paid
buy	bought	put	put
catch	caught	read	read
come	came	ride	rode
cut	cut	say	said
do	did	see	saw
drive	drove	send	sent
eat	ate	set	set
fight	fought	sit	sat
find	found	spend	spent
forget	forgot	take	took
get	got	tell	told
give	gave	think	thought
go	went	understand	understood
grow	grew	wear	wore
have	had	win	won
hear	heard	write	wrote
keep	kept		